# The Guide
# to
# Translation
# and
# Localization

*Preparing Products for the Global Marketplace*

*by*

Library of Congress Number 00-191926
ISBN 0-9703948-0-2

Additional Copies can be ordered from
Lingo Systems
Benjamin Franklin Plaza
One S.W. Columbia, Suite 300
Portland, Oregon 97258
1-800-878-8523
www.lingosys.com
info@lingosys.com

Printed in the United States of America

## Editors

John Watkins - Editor

Jeff Williams - Managing Editor

Clark Hays - Copy Editor

Maria Falasca - Copy Editor

## Art Director

Roger Thompson

## Contributing Writers

Donald Arney, Ting Fan, Rosie Ferdig, Cristina Tacconi Johns, Dan Johnson, Chris van Grunsven, Willy van Grunsven, Ursula Mühlhaus-Moyer, Cédric Vézinet, John Watkins, Laura Williams and Janet Zamecki. And thanks to: Priscella Cheung, Mariken de Jong, Mercedes Edgerton, Rich Radford, Chizuru Sezai, and Barbara Weiss.

## Trademark Information

Windows and Windows Help are trademarks of Microsoft Corporation. TRADOS Translator's Workbench for Windows is the registered trademark of TRADOS GmbH. Quark and QuarkXpress are registered trademarks of Quark, Inc. Adobe, Adobe Illustrator, Adobe Photoshop, Acrobat, FrameMaker, PageMaker, Adobe Type Manager, and PostScript are trademarks of Adobe Systems, Inc.

All other brand or product names, trademarks, service marks, and copyrights are the property of their respective owners.

## Contact Information

Lingo Systems
Benjamin Franklin Plaza
One S.W. Columbia, Suite 300
Portland, Oregon 97258
Tel: 800-878-8523
503-224-2256
FAX: 503-224-3663
www.lingosys.com
info@lingosys.com

Localisation Industry Standards Association (LISA)
7, route du Monastère CH-117 Féchy
Switzerland
Tel: 41 21 821 32 10
Fax: 41 21 821 32 19
lisa@lisa.org
www.lisa.org

# Foreword

I n today's Internet-driven economy, the global market is increasingly becoming the baseline for business.
The Web is leveling the playing field by providing an internationally accessible, technically homogenous platform for the delivery of information and goods in electronic forms. Advertising, marketing, sales, distribution and support now can all take place online in whole or in part—revolutionizing supply chains and bringing entry barriers tumbling down. This represents both an opportunity and a potential threat for businesses, and this situation can only be adequately addressed in a concerted manner. Products and accompanying information of all kinds must be designed for international audiences so that they can be easily tailored to local language and cultural needs.

In this multinational, multilingual context, translation and localization are taking on the status of strategic issues, rather than more or less optional afterthoughts. Globalization is becoming more than just a buzzword. It reflects how you will position your company in the global/local marketplace so that your enterprise can reap the internal and external benefits of operating internationally. The value added by multilingual solutions providers in this area—from consulting on specific markets, product and process design, to production services and customer support—can often make the difference between economic success and failure.

In just ten years, localization has gone from a handful of small translation agencies to a multibillion-dollar global industry. Its international association, LISA, has evolved from a small group of software developers and service suppliers to a resource organization that helps establish standards, promote best practices and educate the market. The growth of the association and the industry is largely due to the technical and business influence of its members.

Nevertheless, much confusion prevails about what is needed to ensure successful globalization, and how these requirements should be organized. It is here that a publication such as *The Guide to Translation and Localization* can help. By offering pragmatic advice, it helps companies going global for the first time, as well as those who are trying new techniques or changing production models, to shorten the learning curve. LISA is proud to be associated with this work, and wishes its producers every success.

Michael Anobile,
Managing Director
Localisation Industry Standards Association (LISA)

## John Watkins

*"People say that, sooner or later, you begin to resemble the person with whom you live. My roommate is a French Bulldog."*

# Welcome to the World of Product Translation and Localization!

This is our third edition of *The Guide to Translation and Localization*. This book began as a means to educate our clients on the processes of translation and localization. The high demand for the first edition of our book led to the publication of the second edition. This book was updated and then published for a wider distribution. Now, a year later, we are updating the book once again, so that you can have access to the latest information in the localization industry. We are delighted to be co-publishing this book with LISA (the Localisation Standards Industry Association). LISA fills a vital role in the ongoing development of localization standards, helping to lead all of us in the industry forward into the emerging global economy.

This compendium of translation and localization guidelines is written by our staff to give you an overview of the many facets of our industry. We combined forces to provide guidance on each aspect of the localization industry: from procuring localization support to understanding software user interface and Web site localization. Of course, to address all aspects of translation and localization in detail would require thousands of pages, and probably not be particularly interesting to the "newcomer" to localization. Learning should be fun, and to be fun, we have kept our chapters short and easy to understand. Our easy-to-read guide shows how you can successfully approach a document translation or software localization project.

This book is not written in "one voice" but, instead, keeps the character of each of the contributors. This allows you to develop a feel for the personalities involved in localization, hopefully making it more personal as you experience the diversity and creativity of our staff through their writings. Pictures of the contributors to the book are scattered throughout the chapters to let you put a face to the names.

Each chapter of the guide stands alone, allowing you to read each section when it is needed. You may find, for example, certain chapters are relevant for your marketing staff, others for your engineering staff, and yet others for procurement. We just hope that you find them all helpful!

We provide a number of translation mistakes that have made it into the industry in our "Oops" pages. These are funny stories of how some translations have gone awry. They have a purpose besides making you laugh, though. They graphically illustrate the importance of using professionals to manage your translation projects. How many times have you chuckled over badly translated installation instructions? Just think—would you like to have someone laughing about your product? Failing to gain market share because your product, or its documentation, "feels" foreign is really not a laughing matter. After investing so much to develop your products, you shouldn't allow them to be downgraded in their international versions.

Enjoy your journey into the world of translation and localization. If we can be of any help to you, please just ask.

Sincerely,

John Watkins
Chief Operating Officer
Lingo Systems

*Pepsi's "Come Alive With the Pepsi Generation" was translated into "Pepsi Brings Your Ancestors Back From the Grave" in Chinese.*

*The Coca-Cola name in China was first read as "Kekoukela", meaning "Bite the wax tadpole" or "Female horse stuffed with wax", depending on the dialect. Coke then researched 40,000 characters to find a phonetic equivalent "kokou kole", translating into "happiness in the mouth."*

# Learning the Lingo

Alvin Toffler coined the term "future shock" in the 1970s and Faith Popcorn gave us the word "cocooning" in the 1980s. No such inventor is known for words like "globalization," "internationalization," "localization," "translation," and "interpretation." Yet understanding these terms and their corresponding activities is a critical first step in product development. You may run into some people using these terms in different ways, but here is how we use them:

- **Globalization**: The process of designing your product for the global marketplace so that it can be sold anywhere in the world with only minor revision. It is most easily thought of as your global marketing strategy.

- **Internationalization**: The process of engineering a product so that it can be easily and efficiently localized. Engineering can take the form of something as basic as document layout, for example. When you design the pages of your document, leave plenty of white space so that text expansion can be easily accommodated. From a software perspective, internationalization can mean writing source code so that it handles the different date formats and character encoding necessary for foreign markets.

- **Localization**: The process of customizing a product for consumers in a target market so that when they use it, they form the impression that it was designed by a native of their own country.

- **Translation**: The process of actually converting the written word of a source language into the written word of a target language. Translation is a crucial component of localization.

- **Interpretation**: The process of converting the spoken word of a source language into the spoken word of a target language.

Globalization is particularly important in consumer industries such as clothing and food. Anyone can drink Coca Cola or wear Levi Strauss jeans, for example. However, the bottle size may need to be adapted to foreign vending machines or the logo on the jeans may need translation. Software, documents, Web sites, and multimedia material must be localized to achieve appreciable market share in individual countries.

To better understand the difference in these terms, assume you are designing a new word processing software. Your product development team likely assembled comments from distributors throughout the world whose customers requested new features for your yet-to-be designed word processor. Your marketing department has determined the global demand for such a product and developed a global branding for it.

You may then internationalize the software by designing it with:

- Culturally neutral screen colors to avoid offending potential customers,

- Dialog boxes wide enough to accommodate text expansion,

- Right justified text fields to prevent expanded text from overlapping the graphics, and

- A readily adaptable user interface to allow British customers to read from left to right or Arabic customers to read from right to left.

Proper internationalization may also lower costs. One software manufacturer found that nearly 50% of all support costs came from consumers in foreign markets who could not understand English documentation.

Selling your word processor in Taiwan may require localizing the user's manual, software, help files, and the software user interface from English into Traditional Chinese. Your marketing effort may require interpreting the sales presentation in Mandarin, the language spoken in Taiwan.

Localizing your product, while sometimes challenging, pays handsome rewards. Major software and hardware manufacturers report that 60% or more of their business revenues are now earned outside the U.S.

By offering your products around the world, in a version that appeals to each locale, your organization can increase its distribution, extend the shelf-life of products, and ultimately be less dependent upon the American market.

*Hunt-Wesson introduced its Big John products in French Canada as "Gros Jos" before finding out that the phrase, in slang, means "big breasts!"*

*Colgate introduced a toothpaste in France named "Cue," the name of a notorious pornographic magazine.*

**Dan Johnson**

*"Being a small part of a big team here at Lingo Systems has its benefits. One is with such a diverse variety of expatriates working here, the breakroom smells absolutely fabulous (and admittedly sometimes just weird) at lunch time. If there's a downside, it's that almost everyone's second or third language is better than mine. It's no wonder they'll never let me translate."*

# Getting Started

Let's sell the Widget V2.0 overseas! OK, how do we have it localized?

Wonderful news—your program manager just informed you that you're going to sell the new Widget V2.0 overseas! To add to the good news, you are in charge of having the documentation, software drivers, Website, online documentation, help files, and printed documentation localized prior to sale in the foreign market. What do you have to do? How are you going to do it? The 'how' and 'what' behind localization can be big questions, indeed.

If you are serious about taking on a localization project of any size, you need to know how to first define exactly what work you need. The next component is asking your prospective localization vendor just what they are capable of doing for you. Just as importantly, you need to know how to tell them what you need. The fourth step involves setting out the scope, timeline, and budget for the localization of your product.

Often times, the biggest challenge in localization is effectively laying out the scope of a localization project. A variety of factors can influence the ultimate success of your project. As localization is often a complex, multi-step process, to ensure a successful project, accurate and realistic decisions about the scope of your localization must be made prior to project start. With a clear understanding of where you want to go, your chances of getting there in one piece are greatly improved.

For simplicity, let's break down the localization process into manageable pieces. With a clear understanding of each component, a project scope can be established. With that in mind, you can then go about selecting the localization method and vendor that best suits your specific needs.

## How much to localize

How many components of your project really need to be localized? This decision can span the continuum from "nothing at all" to "all content in the product components." In many cases, timeline or budget considerations may dictate the amount of content to be localized; however, you must weigh the impacts of not localizing content. Impacts can span from the possibility of offending a target market by not providing information in a language that they understand to being restricted by regulations from distributing products that are not localized for the target country. In fact, with the current trend towards globalization of our economy, it's prudent to consult with the appropriate authorities about the legal implications of not localizing some content. As just about anything can be localized, you need to consider the options, with an eye always on the ultimate cost and timeframe necessary for localization.

The decision of how many languages to translate is frequently driven by market necessity, market demand, and/or regulatory needs. Fortunately, the more languages that can be translated at one time, the more efficient the process can be from both a timeline and cost perspective.

## What needs to be localized?

Depending upon the components of your product, you may be localizing the software user interface (UI), help files, legal warranties, last minute "readme" files, and product documentation. That's not to mention the customer support information on your Web site and the training materials used by your international office to train end users. Of course, marketing and customer support are updating the Web content weekly and you have to also consider "roll outs" of product revisions every six months.

Fortunately, localization of many of these components benefits from some of the newer techniques and technologies applied to content management. Recently, tools and methodologies have been developed to enhance the re-use of content across many different media types.

## Getting the parts together

With all the various parts involved in a product, you have to think about the order that things should be submitted for localization. If your documentation has 20 screen captures from the software UI, the UI needs to be localized before the documentation is localized (or at least before it is finalized for printing!). Since Help files often link directly to the software and also contain screen captures, the UI had better get done first. Fortunately, components such as training material and Web content can wait until the bulk of the product localization is complete—after all, they can't train the users until you have something for them to train on!

## You want it when?

There are two typical approaches for global marketing: Target the US and foreign markets simultaneously or launch the English and develop target markets on an "as needed" basis. Both approaches can negatively impact your localization timeline. Assuming you are choosing simultaneous release, you have to localize your English content while they are still making modifications to it. That's what change orders are for...

So, localizing after the English is complete and target markets request your product must be easier, right? On one hand it is—the English content is at least stable. Unfortunately, your sales team needs to have the products localized in five days because the new market is screaming for it. That is what rush charges are for...

**TIPS**

If possible, separate any text from your graphics (either as call-outs or separate layers). It makes localization much easier!

On a serious note, it is truly just a matter of planning and setting realistic expectations. If you go for simultaneous release, an iterative development lifecycle can help you achieve that. You provide your localization vendor with the "alpha" or "beta" version of the software and then, when you go to functional complete, they can finalize the translations. It means a little more work, but everything is finished at the same time. If you choose to do a delayed release, localizing your components as they are needed, you can lay the groundwork with your vendor so that the components are "ready to roll" through the production process as soon as you give the go-ahead.

## What does that mean?

Your vendor has been reviewing all the content for localization and is stumped. What is a Widget Whirlygig? Here is where the glossary comes into play. If you are in an industry that uses very specialized terms, you may be asked to provide your localization vendor with a list of terms and their meanings. Your vendor is probably pretty smart, so if you are using standard terms from the software, automotive, medical, construction, etc. industry, you may not need to do anything. They can create a terminology list, instead. The main difference here is that a terminology list does not need to provide definitions of the terms because everyone knows what they are. In either case, whether for a glossary or a terminology list, the time put into their development pays off down the road with more consistent use of terminology from one translation to the next.

# What, me worry?

## Domestic vs overseas vendors

You may be tempted to use your overseas office to localize your product. They speak the language, after all, so how much easier that would be! While it is true that localizing overseas in the target country may allow better target market knowledge, it can also lead to other problems such as:

• Less control from headquarters,

• Risks to schedule,

• Incorrect translations due to lack of knowledge of latest US technology, and

• Difficult communications with engineers and documentation staff due to differences in time zones, especially near the project end where rapid changes often take place.

At a recent STC (Society for Technical Communication) conference we heard the story of one company's experience with their overseas vendor. The overseas vendor had not maintained open lines of communication, ultimately failing to meet release dates and, to add insult to lateness, used unapproved artwork. The product had to be pulled off the shelf and redone. This company lost 12 weeks of marketing time, not to mention thousands upon thousands of dollars.

This is certainly an extreme example, and by no means are all overseas vendors unreliable. It merely indicates the importance of knowing the special requirements of working with vendors who are located in different time zones.

Usually a combination of both is best: coordinate the localization efforts in the US to ease communication but involve your overseas office or an overseas contact in preparing terminology lists before translation and in reviewing the translation before it is delivered.

Now you have to decide whether to handle individual translators yourself or to use a full-service localization vendor to manage your localization efforts. The issue here is one of price versus quality. Do you have the time and staff to hire and manage translators and determine the quality of their results? A full-service vendor can provide you with all the resources necessary for you to receive a quality translation on time and on budget.

**TIPS**

Avoid using slang terms. Slang is difficult to translate and does not always work in the target country.

## Getting an estimate

Once you have located potential vendors, you must communicate your needs to them (typically to their client account manager). As you begin your discussions, the vendor representative should pose many questions to you before trying to send you an estimate of the project. Preparing your information in concise, easy to follow units, makes this transfer of requirements easier. Once each potential vendor has the information they need, an estimate can be generated for you so that you can pick the lucky winner.

So now, armed with a bunch of estimates—how do you make heads or tails out of them? Comparing one bid to another is not an easy task. It's tempting to accept the offer of a few bids from different vendors and then to simply go with the lowest bid. Resist that temptation! Take the time to investigate each vendor's services thoroughly. Here is a list of questions you can use to interview a potential vendor:

- What is your company's area of specialization?

- How do you qualify your linguists?

- How will you manage my project?

- Will I receive status reports on my project?

- Who will be my primary contact during the project?

- Do you have the necessary hardware and software to efficiently handle my work?

- Have you managed projects like mine before?

- How do you assure quality?

- Will you develop and maintain a terminology list specific to my project?

- How are changes handled during the course of a project?

- What is your record for delivering on time?

- How accurate are your estimates?

- Can you provide me with references and examples of similar completed projects?

Every good localization vendor should be able to give you an accurate estimate based on a clearly defined pricing structure. The chart below is a sample pricing structure describing basic services and how they may be billed.

| Project level | Price |
|---|---|
| Project management | Typically 10-15% of total costs |

| Documentation | Price |
|---|---|
| Translation | Per word or per page |
| Copy edit | Per word or per page or hour |
| Proofread | Per hour |
| Glossary/terminology development | Per hour |
| Desktop publishing | Per hour or per page |
| Output of film or RC paper, etc. | Per page |
| Quality assurance | Per hour |

## Software, Web site, & online documentation

| Software, Web site, & online documentation | Price |
| --- | --- |
| Translation, copy edit, proof | Same as for documentation |
| Glossary/terminology Development | Same as for documentation |
| Desktop publishing | Same as for documentation |
| Screenshots | Per screen shot or per hour |
| Engineering | Per hour |
| Functional testing | Per hour |
| Graphics and screen captures | Per hour |
| Exact match | No charge |
| Fuzzy match | Flat charge per word or phrase |
| New strings/sentences | Per word |
| Translation memory administration | Per hour |

Taking the time to select a localization partner with the skills and resources to meet your needs not only save you time and money for your current projects, but ideally, also leads to the development of a long-term partnership. The value of a long-term relationship between client and vendor cannot be overemphasized. It provides the means for your vendor to know you and your product well. The better your vendor understands you and your product line, the more smoothly the localization process can proceed, and project management and communication protocols can be fine-tuned. The long-term relationship between client and localization vendor is, ultimately, the best way to achieve quality work for each and every project.

*Outside a Paris dress shop a sign declared: Dresses for street walking.*

***In a Swiss mountain inn:*** *Special today - no ice cream.*

**Ursula Mühlhaus-Moyer**

*"Frequently my responsibilities at Lingo Systems permit me to travel the globe via cyberspace to develop and nurture linguistic resources. Less frequently, I am privileged to meet first hand with our "partners" across the nation and the continents. Besides the reward of personal connection, the opportunity to learn about cultures and history and to travel, by all means, keeps the drive alive."*

# Linguistic Quality through Terminology

To achieve the highest linguistic quality, the localization process must include the development of:

- A style guideline,

- A glossary in the source language, and

- A terminology list in the target language.

While these steps add time to the production initiation phase, when done properly they save a greater amount of time during the translation phase while simultaneously enabling a higher quality result and ensure consistency in the translation of all components of the localized product.

## What are style guidelines?

Style guidelines, or style sheets, are writing guidelines the linguist can follow during the translation process. They are either provided by the client or are developed by the linguist in coordination with the client. Guidelines can address the following issues:

- Tone of the localized documentation,

- Those terms that are translated, and those that are not,

- Rules for capitalization and accent marks,

- Translation of titles and subtitles,

- Conversion of measurements,

- Rules for spelling numbers,

- Use of abbreviations, and

- Punctuation rules.

The quality of the localized documentation is largely dependent upon the quality of the source text. Therefore, it is important that the technical writer knows in advance that the documentation is to be translated. It can be beneficial to have the technical writer initially work with the localization vendor to ensure that the subsequent documentation is created for a global audience, that cultural and other country-specific issues are addressed early in the process, and that specific steps are taken to ease the translation process.

Style guidelines should be developed based upon the consensus of the client, the in-country evaluator and the localization vendor. This helps to create documents appropriate to the user-level, and meet company and country standards as well as maintain local and cultural suitability.

## What is a glossary?

A glossary is a list of words in the source language in which difficult or technical, product-specific terms are explained. Typically, the glossary is developed by the technical writers and software engineers who are working on your specific project.

## What is a terminology list?

A terminology list is an agreed-upon list of terms, in the target language, to be used in the localization process. It ensures:

- Consistency of linguistic processes throughout the project (i.e., that they all work with the same terms), covering product, industry, and user interface terms, for use in all of the components,

- Consistency of abbreviations, product names, nontranslated terms, and measurements,

- Consistency between country and company standards,

- Local suitability, and

- Consensus among client, distributor, and localization provider.

The terminology is based on:

- The product-specific glossary developed by the technical writer of the source document,

- The localized user interface terminology of major software developers,

- Prior localized software and documentation, and

- All other localized resource materials such as marketing collateral, product lists, as well as company and country standards.

Company "standards" are ways of referring to specific things or specific documents that are unique to the particular company and include part numbers, technical and product support information, warranties, license agreements, copy rights, references to other software, product names, brand names, and nonlocalized components.

Country "standards" are ways of expressing functional or cultural dictates, such as publishing standards, sorting of lists, abbreviations, time, dates, holidays, currency, and measurements.

**TIPS**

Try to choose fonts that are available on both MAC and PC platforms.

In order to match the company and country standards, and to make sure that there is consistency and accuracy between software and documentation, the terminology list must be developed early on in the localization process before the actual translation begins.

## Who establishes, updates, and validates the terminology list?

The lead linguist on your project develops the terminology list. The lead gathers all resource materials and consults as needed with the product developers to obtain explanations of any ambiguous terms (this may be facilitated by the project manager of your localization vendor). The linguistic lead also updates and validates the list systematically throughout the localization process. The terminology list is then used by each of the linguists in the multistep translation. If any additions, deletions, or modification of the terminology list are suggested, they are funneled back to the lead linguist for verification first.

## What if the terminology list was not developed?

There are countless examples in which one word in a target language can correctly be translated into several equally valid terms. The lead linguist and the client need to agree which term or terms are appropriate in their specific circumstances. Certain terms can vary depending on whether the term refers to software or hardware, or whether it is being presented in a formal, informal, or imperative context. Some terms may not even be translatable, or may be referred to by an abbreviation based on the English term or the translated term.

## Examples in Spanish

- **Agreement on terminology**

  *Congratulations* can be translated correctly into *Felicitaciones* or *Enhorabuena*.

- **Local suitability**

  *Congratulations!* as well as *Welcome to .....* is frequently used in user manuals to introduce a new product. Should the Spanish audience be addressed in this rather colloquial American way? Is there a more formal way to address the user, or should this greeting not be used at all?

- **Abbreviation**

  *UK* — Siglas en inglés (United Kingdom) de *Reino Unido*

In all cases the abbreviation is written first, with the name for which it stands written in parentheses. However, there appears to be no set standard on the placement of the translated text. Client and localization vendor need to agree if the translated text should be placed immediately after the abbreviation or after the name for which it stands.

## Examples in German

- **Variation between software and hardware terminology**

*Set up* is translated into *Einrichten* if the term refers to setting up the software and *Anschließen* if the term refers to setting up a peripheral device.

- **Non-translated terms**

In projects where the documentation is translated but the user interface stays in English, there should be an agreement about whether the English term is followed by the potential localized term in parentheses or vice versa.

*Klicken Sie auf Load/Unload Panel (Stück laden/Entfernen),* or

*Klicken Sie auf Stück laden/Entfernen (Load/Unload Panel)*

- **Style**

*Connect your printer to the computer* can be translated formally into:

*Schließen Sie den Drucker an den Computer an.*

Or in imperative voice:

*Drucker an den Computer anschließen.*

Or in passive voice:

*Der Drucker muss an den Computer angeschlossen werden.*

## Examples in Japanese

Depending on the platform, commands and buttons are translated differently:

| English | Japanese Macintosh | Japanese Windows |
| --- | --- | --- |
| Save As | 別名保存 | 名前を付けて保存 |
| Cut | 切り取り | カット |
| Print | 印刷 | プリント |

**TIPS**

Avoid packing text too tightly on your dialog boxes, as it is likely to expand when the controls are localized.

**Jeff Williams**

*"I have many international friends, but my favorite by far is Evita Bezuidenhout, formerly Evita Goldfarb of Flatbush, New York. Evita defied her parents, who wanted her to go into the family candle business, and married a Dutch puppeteer named Sjaak Bezuidenhout. Evita and Sjaak live happily on a leaky boat on a canal in Valkenswaard, Holland. I have learned a lot about life from Evita."*

Depending on the context, an English word can be translated into multiple terms in the target language:

| English | Japanese |
|---|---|
| Address | アドレス、　住所 |
| Title | 題名、　タイトル、　呼称 |
| Class | クラス、　級、　レベル、　（授業） |
| Time | 時間、　タイム |

On the other hand, some multiple terms can be translated into a single term:

| English | Japanese |
|---|---|
| Tall | 高い |
| High | 高い |
| Expensive | 高い |
| Pretentious | 高い |

Some words and abbreviations, by convention, stay in English:

| | |
|---|---|
| lpi | lines per inch |
| pts | points |
| m/cm/mm | meter/centimeter/millimeter |
| kg/g/mg | kilogram/gram/milligram |

## Conclusions

Costly rework of the localized content can result if style guidelines, glossary, and the terminology list are not developed, are used too late in the project, or are used but not approved by your companies in-country representatives. Early clarification saves linguistic, software engineering—and project management time. With a carefully developed and managed terminology, all linguistic team members work from the same resource material. Time consuming and costly communication between project managers, technical specialists, the client and in-country evaluators are avoided and the project progresses smoothly. If style guidelines and terminology are based on the consensus of all parties involved, the client, distributor, and localization vendor are pleased with their localized product and the groundwork for future successful work together has been laid.

**Leaflet handed out to vacationers at Palma airport, Mallorca:**

*Distinguished visitor:*

*It is known that all the turistic services in Mallorca are maintaining a correct relation price quality, but even though, we wish to prize the establishments and services that to the opinion of our visitors, surpass notoriously for their quality.*

*To be able to fill out these questionnaires you must write the name of this establishment, installation or turistic service, as is shown below, and you must give a punctuation between 6 and 10 points hoping that the service that you must punctuate has been the best in the relation price-quality.*

*Ford had a problem in Brazil when the Pinto flopped. The company found out that Pinto was Brazilian slang for "tiny male parts." Ford pried all the nameplates off and substituted Corcel, which means horse.*

**In a Belgrade hotel elevator:**

*To more the cabin, push button for wishing floor. If the cabin should enter more persons, each one should press a number of wishing floor. Driving is then going alphabetically by national order.*

# Working with Fonts, Layouts and Graphics

When selecting fonts for a new document destined for translation, remember that simpler is better. Different languages contain a multitude of accents and special characters, highlighting the need for font legibility. Avoid ornate or decorative fonts. The conventional combination of a standard serif font (e.g.—Times) for body copy and a standard sans serif font (e.g.—Helvetica) for headings is a good example of font selections that work well for translation. In general, stick to fonts that are clean and crisply drawn, avoiding fonts with exceptionally thin serifs or wispy detail.

Try to keep the total number of fonts used in the document to a manageable number—no more than three or four. Ideally, select fonts that are available on both PC and Macintosh platforms. This facilitates the easy movement of the document across platforms, if required, during localization.

Most Western European or English fonts (e.g.—Helvetica and Times) contain an extended character set that provides accented letters, such as "í." However, Central European languages contain characters not included in these commonly used fonts. If a document is targeted for Central European languages, it is important to choose fonts that have a matching CE version such as Helvetica CE or Times CE. Your localization vendor can help you research and locate a font set that is appropriate for the look and feel of your document.

## Asian languages and separate operating systems

Many other languages require special fonts that are not available as extended character sets. Several even require separate operating systems. For example, Japanese, Korean, Traditional and Simplified Chinese are considered "double-byte languages." This means each written character contains two bytes (16 bits) of data instead of 1 byte (8 bits). This causes problems for applications and operating systems that do not support double-byte characters. The shift in character encoding to unicode should help this problem, but we are not there yet.

Character styles used in Western European or US English layouts do not always translate into Asian languages. In many cases they are not used at all. Character styles such as bold and italic are not always applicable to Asian type styles. Furthermore, Asian characters do not distinguish between upper- and lowercase. For design purposes, the best way to distinguish Asian characters from surrounding text is to vary the font face or weight (e.g.—using a heavier version of a typeface for added emphasis). Your localization vendor has a variety of techniques to help keep the look and feel in your Asian product as you originally intended.

# Layouts

I t is vitally important that your document's layout leaves enough room (i.e.—white space) for the inevitable text expansion that occurs during the localization process. This cannot be overemphasized: formatting of the translated document is far easier and more efficient when adequate space is available. Formatting costs can rise dramatically when the translated text must be laboriously manipulated to fit within a cramped space.

As a general rule of thumb, allow for 20 to 30 percent expansion of your English text when it is translated. It is best to be conservative, using the 30 percent figure whenever possible, resulting in an English document that contains a fair amount of white space (something that is, in fact, desirable). In technical documentation, there is a tendency to make pages too dense and crowded, impairing the readability and hence comprehension of the material presented. This extra white space makes your English that much more readable!

In addition to allowing for text expansion, you also need to decide whether or not you want hyphenation used in your document. The use of hyphenation affects the expansion of the translated text on a page. Non-hyphenated text generally takes up more space on a page due to the limited opportunity for convenient line breaks.

Perhaps most importantly, for technical support considerations, decide whether the translated documents should maintain the same page breaks and the same total number of pages as the English document. It is generally easier, and therefore less expensive, if page breaks can change during the localization process. From the perspective of customer support, however, it is often preferable for the localized manuals to match the page breaks of the English so that support can always refer to "page 37 of the manual" for solving a problem. If page break matching is desired, it is even more important to allow for the "extra white space" described above. Matching page breaks from source to target documents can add to the cost of the project, especially when the source document does not allow sufficient white space for text expansion.

When you are ready to hand off your product to a localization vendor, always provide a hardcopy with the electronic files. This allows the vendor to double-check that the localized files match the electronic file you provided. It is all too easy to accidentally hand off the wrong revision, or version, of a product for localization.

**TIPS**

A computer-assisted translation tool can help you assess how much time and money you can save via leveraging.

**Janet Zamecki**

*"Can't talk...have a deadline. No, really...I have a deadline! OK! I fell into computers and I can't speak any language other than English, which is amazing considering I took 12 years of Spanish. But I know how to format! Boy, do I know how to format! And I get to format all I want to at Lingo Systems!"*

# Graphics

Ideally, graphics should not contain text for the simple reason that this eliminates any need for translation in those files. If text must be associated with a graphic, try to create the text as a separate component in the page-layout application (e.g., FrameMaker, QuarkXpress) used to create the document. That is, a callout or caption for a graphic should ideally be a text block in the layout program, not an element of an Illustrator Encapsulated Postscript (EPS) file. This requires less work to localize (saving you money), as the graphic text is part of the main document test and not a layer inside the graphic file.

If you must include text in the EPS graphic files, remember to leave it in text form. Do not outline the text, as this makes it very difficult and time-consuming to retype and translate any words in the graphic.

Screen shots are a special category of graphics. By their very nature, they contain text. Translation of screen shot text is accomplished through localization of the software that was used to generate the English shots, followed by regeneration of the screen shots using the localized software. When creating applications, be aware of how the text fits in various windows. As with printed documents, avoid packing text too tightly, as it expands when the software is localized (please see the chapter on software localization). When creating the screen shots in English, be sure to generate all of them at the same screen resolution and scale, saving the graphics file in the same file format used by the document layout application.

## Preparing files for HTML or PDF conversion

Many companies are making their documentation available to customers not just in a paper-based medium, but also in an electronic form (such as the HTML or PDF formats). These two formats are widely used on the Internet and on electronic media (e.g., distribution CDs) because they appear virtually the same regardless of the operating system the customer uses to view them. They also have the advantage of avoiding printing and distribution charges for hardcopy manuals. For complex, inter-related documents, they also offer the advantage of incorporating hypertext—clicking on a cross-reference, index, or table of contents entry takes the user immediately to the relevant entry, an important savings of time and effort.

Previously, a customer support page, like a company's Web site, would have to be made from scratch. Fortunately, most word-processing or layout programs currently have or are soon implementing support for direct conversion of existing files into HTML or PDF format.

This means that a document can be exported into one of these formats easily, retaining a layout and style in keeping with the print edition (useful for purposes of version control, as well as for maintaining a uniform company style throughout the documents).

Though this method may offer substantial savings in time, effort, and money, it also requires careful preparation when going into the process. The advice on font selection given earlier also applies to electronic documentation. While English and most other Western European languages can use the same font system that is used to encode HTML and PDF files, many other languages require special care.

On a more nuts-and-bolts level, both HTML and PDF files incorporate and, to a certain extent require, style tags. HTML uses nothing but style markers to instruct browsers how to format text. The use of style tags is not an integral component of PDF files, but it aids the generation process of such useful features as bookmarks.

Whether converting your documentation to HTML or PDF format, your document headings convey the same structured sense of importance incorporated in the print document. A document that does not use style tags efficiently (for example, uses a different style tag each time, to produce exactly the same formatting attributes), requires much more time to set up than a document that uses only one style tag to represent this uniform style. Using consistent style definitions throughout your document allows both PDF bookmark data and HTML style tags to be generated in the localized files more easily.

*Japan's second-largest tourist agency was mystified when it entered English-speaking markets and began receiving requests for unusual romantic tours. Upon finding out why, the owners of Kinki Nippon Tourist Company changed its name.*

## Cédric Vézinet

*"I have done some crazy things in my life. From skydiving to bungee-jumping, from martial arts to commando training camp. I will not even give you the details on the drinking games we have in southern France. The interesting thing is that I have done all that without a single physical injury, but since I was hired at Lingo Systems ..."*

# Translation Tools

Using a machine to do translation seems like a great idea. It can be cost effective and shorten the time needed to localize a product. We have to be careful, however, before reaching conclusions about the quality and efficiency of machine translation vs. human translation. Translating is not simply about replacing one word with another, it's a mental and emotional process that includes feelings, cultural differences, understanding of the target country—and so on. These are areas in which machines are likely to never surpass human beings. Also, since language is a living thing that is constantly evolving, it is notoriously hard to keep translation programs current. When a machine translates a document by itself, it can result in enormous misinterpretations and misunderstandings—mistakes that can cost you your reputation (not to mention money). That's why it's more efficient to rely on machines for some level of support, but not to count on them to do the entire job for you. And, to be honest, there are some great machine translation tools out there!

There are three major categories of tools to assist or automate the translation process: terminology managers, machine translation tools, and computer assisted translation tools (CAT).

## Terminology managers

The function of a terminology manager is to store the source terminology and the corresponding target terminology. The terminology manager either inserts the translated terms contained in its database while the linguist is working on a document, or gives a warning signal before inserting the target language term. This kind of tool is interesting, but allows only a limited degree of user flexibility and in the end is little more than an on-line dictionary.

## Machine translation tools

Machine translation tools (MTs), on the other hand, take care of the whole translation process for you. MTs are based on advanced computational linguistic analysis. Once again, however, MTs may present some problems.

In order to have the MT translate a document, it must be free of typographic errors, misspelled words, and grammatical errors. Those factors influence the way the machine understands the text and translates it. Yes, those machines are pretty smart, but apparently not smart enough to cope with mistakes. In fairness though, these tools are useful for someone who needs to understand the general meaning of a document without caring about having a high-quality translation. This type of translation is now referred to as a "gist" translation—it gives you the gist of the meaning.

Although experienced translators can use MT tools very effectively, the use of fully automatic MTs by an inexperienced person (one who is not a professional translator) can lead to situations where the quality of the translation is laughable at best, insulting at worst. Here are some examples (Spanish to English) of what can happen when a professional translator, fully apprised of the limitations of machine translation, is not involved in the translation process:

| Spanish | Original English | MT Translation into English |
|---------|------------------|-----------------------------|
| Usar la Vara Escribe... | using the Wand Pen... | Use the stick writes |
| Barrida la pluma ladea rápidamente y fácilmente por el entero obstruye codificatión. | Sweep the pen tip quickly and smoothly across the entire barcode. | Swept the pen tilts quickly and easily by the entire obstructs codification. |
| Un muy toque de la luz es todo lo que requiere. | A very light touch is all you need. | A very touch of the light is all it requires. |

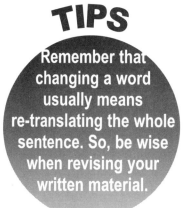

**TIPS**
Remember that changing a word usually means re-translating the whole sentence. So, be wise when revising your written material.

While these translation examples are somewhat humorous, it is important to realize the repercussions. In the wrong hands, machine translation can be catastrophic for your image.

To effectively use machine translation in your localization process, you must plan for it from the beginning and expend the resources necessary to have the best quality source materials and translation tools. The English content must be written to exacting standards; no fancy wording is allowed! Most organizations that use machine translation successfully report the development of "stylized English" that must be used by the technical writers in generating content. Using stylized English allows the machine translation developers to establish customized databases and grammar rules for each target language, improving the quality of the resulting translation. Even so, the machine-translated text must still be reviewed by human linguists to ensure quality.

## Computer assisted translation (CAT)

Computer assisted translation tools (CAT) are much more useful to linguists and offer an efficient way to improve the speed and quality of translation work. These tools combine a terminology manager and a translation memory which work together. The program stores every sentence or phrase translated by the linguist and offers the previous translation wherever that combination of words (or a similar combination) is found in the current document. The linguist can accept the previous translation or create a new one. The linguist always retains control, but the machine does what machines are good at— automating what can be automated.

You might wonder how this kind of tool could help you. Well, it is important that terminology remain consistent within your document or product as well as from one document or product to another. We have all seen user guides, software, or marketing pieces where this was not done properly and outdated terminology was used, or terms varied inappropriately from one page to another. The CAT tool changes all that. The CAT tool can analyze your electronic files and quickly reveal how much text can be leveraged; that is, how many words do not have to be translated again. You may find that you only need 75% of your new text translated. (Note: even when you use a CAT tool, it is still necessary to copy-edit and proofread the entire text to assure quality.)

Once a glossary is created (the glossary can be imported directly or established throughout the translation process), the translator works on his or her word processor and the CAT tool displays the text that has previously been translated. The translator can then decide to accept the proposed translation or not; it is essential not to impose a translation on the linguists.

Does this make the translation process cheaper? On the first job the answer is—maybe! The reduced translation costs may be offset by the costs of CAT tool administration. If there is a great deal of repetition in the new files, however, the savings could be substantial. Even though there may be more up-front costs for a first time project, the results of the translation are improved—and so the value to you is clearly improved. Even if you want to have the first release of your product localized (a circumstance in which you do not have any previous text to use for leveraging), you may consider using the CAT tools anyway. It is more time consuming (and therefore more expensive) to create a translation memory from previously translated material than to build it automatically during the translation process. By using the CAT tool from the beginning, when you upgrade or introduce a similar product the CAT tool automatically leverages the previously translated text and, in almost every case, your costs are dramatically reduced.

The cost of the translation is also influenced by the different file conversions that may be involved. There are formatting issues to consider, depending on the tools used during the translation process. The original source files you deliver to your translation agency might need to be "cleaned up" to use the CAT tools efficiently. It makes sense for you to coordinate with your vendor's Translation Tools Manager in order to know what you can do to deliver your files in the best possible shape. This means you don't have to pay the translation agency for basic formatting of the source document that can easily be done in-house. For example, when using the Translator's Workbench for Windows with FrameMaker documents, the necessary conversion process from MIF (Maker Interchange Format) files to RTF files can only take place if the hyphenation is turned off and if there are no change bars in the files.

The use of soft returns in the middle of sentences is a problem as well since they are converted as tags and will cut off sentences in the RTF files, making the translation process much more difficult.

The ideal situation is to finalize the source document once you have consulted your vendor to learn the specifics of file formats and document formatting requirements. The bottom line is to save money (as always) and to avoid costly localization problems while achieving the highest quality translation possible.

**At a new nightspot in Russia:**

*A friendly but effective metal detector as well as some other devices are going to ensure that you are safe and sound while you go through all the excitements of the night.*

*One of the longest bars in Moscow meets you a floor above where over 800 sq. m. are at your disposal for tet-a-tet dinner or weird dancing on the cherry stained floor while posh ladies in vivid dresses and immaculate men will be a pleasant view for your eyes. Wait till after midnight the life show will start with hot pop star invited to perform.*

***In a Czechoslovakian tourist agency:*** *Take one of our horse-driven city tours-we guarantee no miscarriages.*

**Laura Williams**

*"One of my favorite aspects of the localization industry is working with people from different countries. The best is when we meet face to face for the first time and feel like old friends."*

# Documentation Project Management

When localizing your documentation, there are many factors to consider. What level of localization suits your needs? For what purpose is the translation to be used? Who is your target audience? Is it an internal document, or is it a product that is being distributed to customers? Your localization vendor can help you determine these needs. Once a decision is reached, the localization project manager can make sure those needs are met.

## Getting started

When beginning a documentation project, it is very important to agree on the project scope with your localization vendor. Establishing a clear scope helps avoid problems, and additional charges for unanticipated changes, once the project gets underway. Your localization vendor should submit a list of questions that range from basic formatting issues to more complicated linguistic issues. The more questions you can answer, the smoother the localization process is for you.

Localization consulting is another service that may be offered by your localization vendor. A localization consultant can assist your company in determining how to best develop your product so that it is easiest to localize. This moves into the arena of internationalization—preparing your products for subsequent localization. For example, guidelines on how to format your documentation so that it is more easily localized may be tailored specifically for your project.

## Terminology

Your product terminology is a critical component that is used extensively by your localization vendor. This translated list of industry and product-specific terminology, along with previously translated documentation you may have, form an excellent starting point for your localization project. It also contributes to consistency in tone between different documents from your company. If your documentation is written based on a software application, it is important for your localization vendor to translate these components first, in order to match the terminology in the documentation. If such material is not available, you can ask your localization vendor to develop and translate a glossary for you before the project starts.

## Formatting

Most documentation today requires formatting to smoothly integrate text flow, graphics, and images. Due to text expansion of most translated languages, your localization vendor needs to know if it is necessary for the formatter to match the page breaks in the source document with those in the target language. If your company normally uses a special font for documentation, you may need to select appropriate alternative fonts for languages that do not have a Roman alphabet. You must also consider what format your graphics are in, whether or not text is mixed with the graphics and how the graphics are placed in the document (by reference or embedded).

## Communication

Communication is the cornerstone of successful project management in any field. In translation and localization work, the client manager (CM) and the project manager (PM) are two key players in all communications between your company and the team your localization vendor assembles to complete your project.

This team may include a key contact person, an in-country reviewer (who can offer advice on terminology and style for your target countries), and a technical expert who can answer questions about the technical specifications discussed in your source document.

It is important to clearly communicate your expected delivery dates, delivery format, and media at the beginning of the project. Similarly, your localization team should communicate expected delivery dates and any issues that need to be resolved back to you. Typically, the localization vendor determines the timeline at the project start, based upon the availability of linguistic and technical resources. The PM or the CM should confirm the anticipated delivery date with you so that all expectations are met.

Remember, you know your product better than anyone else does, and your localization vendor appreciates receiving as much support information as possible ahead of time. This could include anything that may be helpful for a translator to understand your product better such as previous glossaries, terminology lists, or product descriptions, for example.

Establish a clear and thorough communication protocol with both your localization vendor's client manager and project manager. This allows all questions or issues that arise during the project to be dealt with in an effective and timely manner. In the event that you are away from your office while your document is being localized, always bring your replacement up to speed on the project's progress and be sure to let your localization vendor's PM know whom to contact with questions while you are away.

**TIPS**

Developing a glossary helps to guarantee the accuracy and correct usage of technical and industry jargon throughout the translation.

## During the project

Your vendor's CM or PM should keep you informed of the status of your project via e-mail, phone, or fax based on your requested method and frequency of status reports.

Although the majority of projects involve localizing a document that has already been finalized in English, occasionally you may need to change or modify the source document. Frequent changes during the course of a project can become expensive and severely impact the original timeline. For example, if you need a very quick turnaround time for your changes, you might incur rush charges. Communicate clearly what, where, and when these changes are to be made so that your vendor can quickly incorporate them into the final product. Either you or your vendor can choose to maintain the "master English" copy, keeping it up-to-date with all the changes, allowing for the final localized versions to be checked against the "latest" English version.

Changes to the original project scope may cause an increase in localization costs and/or a delay in delivery. Your vendor's CM or PM should submit an estimate for each new change, subject to your approval, that addresses both additional costs and any delivery date adjustments that may be necessary prior to incorporating the changes.

## Completing the project

Once your localization vendor has completed your project, the CM or PM should solicit your comments and feedback. Your input is essential to your vendor's efforts to improve service and performance on future projects. Offer a candid critique of areas where your vendor failed to meet your expectations and praise for tasks well done.

**Letter from a hotel manager, France:**
Dear guest,
You make a verbal - farverbal, written, possibly through mediation of a third one, RESERVATION of a room in our hotel. You can depend on our assent, we keep the room free for You from the minute of the entrance of Your room order; we do this even gladly. But the fact of the ORDER and the ASSENT is OBLIGATORY for BOTH!

**Notice in a hotel, Lagos, Nigeria:**
To whom their duty som-times relied for the uses of our crops immediately don't forget before or after your off cut or harvesting any of the raw pastry notice the nursery gardner i/c whoes supplying records through i/c of the hotel manager are being treated.

**From a bar in Austria:**
The comfortable day bar, with its terrace over the valley where everybody feels himself in private, is appreciated by elderly people. After daylight, the evening bar, where music can not be heard in other parts of the castle, receives youngs and olders in a good relaxing atmosphere.

## Rosie Ferdig

*"Born in Vietnam.
Raised in South Dakota.
And I'm still making
changes. My college
professors trained me to
be a clinical researcher,
but I grew to love the
challenge of
experimenting on office-
dwelling co-workers.
Now I have a desk, a
computer, and a crew of
the best Project
Managers in the
business. I've lived in
Seattle (too far north),
Chicago (too far east)
and San Francisco (too
far south). Now I've
found my bearings at
Lingo Systems and a
home in Portland."*

# Software and Web Site Localization Project Management

## What is it?

Localizing software and Web sites is the translation of computer programs, online documentation (such as help files and Web pages), and related applications from a source language into a target language. An example would be translating your marketing Web site for Widgets from English into French, Italian, Spanish, German, and Japanese, so that you can market the product in the country of the target language. Localization means that kids in France grow up using the "Enregistrer sous" command while your kids can choose the "Save As" command. Have you seen the Arabic version of Microsoft Word or Finnish Netscape? How about on-screen instructions for an hp deskjet printer in Thai? These are amazing examples of software that have been successfully localized.

## Why is it demanding?
## Large word counts, many files

One of the major differences between software/Web site and document localization is that, typically, electronic content (be it in software, online documentation, Web sites, or help systems) often has a large volume of words, scattered through many files, that have to be translated. This text can be found in source code, resource files, HTML files, script files, and help content (such as RTF) files that your team of software engineers has undoubtedly spent a large amount of time writing. To actually see all this text, the software has to be "reassembled" before everything can be displayed correctly on the screen. A typical marketing and sales Web site may contain hundreds of HTML files, integrated with thousands of records in a database, not to mention programming script to make up the final product. All of these components must be localized. The terminology across all these components must not only be done quickly but consistently across all the file types. No wonder it gets complicated!

## Timeframe

As is often the case, you may hope to have your software and Web sites released simultaneously in multiple languages. Even more ambitious, you may wish to release the foreign language version at the same time as the original English version because your Korean customers may not want to wait another six months before they can learn about the Korean version of your product. A simultaneous release means that the localization process must start while the program is still under development.

The translation work can usually be completed within several weeks after the program is finalized. The kind of timeframe required is usually very tight. The scenario is comparable to sending twenty workers to reroof your five-bedroom house while simultaneously laying the foundation.

A simultaneous product release requires that development and localization also occur simultaneously. Any changes to the software, such as how and when certain commands are executed, terminology of commands, button names, or warning messages, must then be immediately incorporated into localized versions as they are being translated.

## Why is project management important?

To illustrate the complexity of localization, consider this example: it takes four hours for grandma to knit a vest. So how many grandmas would it take to have four vests knitted in thirty minutes? Though professional linguists/engineers can work in a more organized way than granny does, the simple logistics of which vest should be knitted first, who works on the heart-shaped pockets, where the yellow yarns should be stored, and so on, illustrates the need for effective management and monitoring for a successful vest-knitting venture. In a localization project, the project manager (PM) coordinates and schedules project resources, monitors progress, trouble-shoots issues, and provides necessary information for all personnel to successfully complete the project on time.

# Project management components of a successful localization project

## Starting a project

- **Developing project specifications**: The PM organizes resources and plans the schedule according to client requirements. It is important for the PM to have a clear understanding of your expectations, especially the format of your deliverables, whether certain Quality Assurance (QA) testing should be performed, what deadlines need to be met, and so on.

- **Specifying the time to freeze the software (or Web site, or online documentation)**: In a simultaneous release project, it is very helpful for your localization vendor to know when you are "freezing" development for the release version. This is especially challenging for Web-based projects as content is always evolving.

- **Specifying the build environment**: The build environment must be clearly specified. Sometimes, localization engineers are forced to spend a number of hours determining this on their own, which is then reflected in your invoice. It is much better to provide a "localization kit" that explains your build environment for any compiling your vendor must perform.

**TIPS**

Set up a clear communication protocol with your localization vendor. This allows all questions that arise during the project to be dealt with in an effective and timely manner.

- **Establishing communication lines**: It is essential to work with your localization vendor to establish a communication protocol. Indicate who should be contacted with technical questions or issues, if they arise, and how this communication should take place (telephone, e-mail, etc.). Often, it is a good idea for the localization engineers to communicate directly with your programmers and testers.

## During a project

- **Version control**: Especially when translation is being done parallel to software development, it is essential to keep track of the latest version.

- **Change orders**: While your vendor should be able to accommodate needed changes, keep in mind they can be costly in terms of going over budget and impacting the project schedule. Try to keep changes to a minimum.

- **Tracking changes**: Any changes to both functionality and terminology should be incorporated into localized versions. It is important for your localization vendor's PMs to have a clear idea of what changed, how, and when.

- **Solving issues**: Be prepared to discuss issues concerning your project as they arise. If your vendor needs your input, it could delay the project if you can't be reached.

## At project end

It is very helpful for your localization vendor to get your post-project comments. This helps your vendor provide the best, most customized service for you on your next project.

**Brochure published by the Danish city of Frederikshavn:**

*I am the puppy among Danish towns.*

*Long, lanky and restless, but a very gay chap.*

*Something must happen where I am - and that is the case. Sometimes it is so hectic that I have some trouble in managing it all, but fun is it.*

**English from Japanese products:**

*UCC "DRINK IT BLACK" COFFEE*
*Black coffee has great features which other coffees have never had: Non-sugar.*

*POCARI SWEAT*
*Pocari Sweat is highly recommended as a beverage for such activities as sports, physical labor, after a hot bath, and even as an eye-opener in the morning.*

*NO-BRAND ORANGE PUNCH*
*This light and smooth taste drink is the best refreshment to you. Anytime, anywhere, just like your friend.*

*DYDO COFFEE*
*There's a gallon of deliciousness in every drop.*

## Chris van Grunsven

*"A native Oregonian for 27 years, it's my job to keep track of local to-do's, and bring the homebrew for late night work parties. Every now and then they even let me do some software projects."*

# Software Internationalization and Localization

Bringing your software product to an international market is a two-part process: Software internationalization and localization. Software internationalization prepares your original source code for the localization process while software localization transforms the English (source language) software into one or more target languages, giving the product the look and feel of having been created in the target country. Software, for our purposes here, refers to one of three broad categories of products you may wish to bring to the world market:

- Software user interface (UI),
- Online documentation (such as help files), and
- Web sites (and their associated HTML/SGML pages, scripts, and applets).

## Software Internationalization

Software internationalization is the process of developing (or preparing already developed) software products with the foreign market in mind. There are several issues to consider before the localization of software products, in any of the three categories, can begin. Each subsection below gives tips and pointers to help you through the internationalization process.

## Separate source code from the user interface

How you write your software applications determines how easy they are to translate. The most basic advice is to separate the text that is going to be displayed on the screen from the core program code. While it is certainly easier to write code with error messages and button labels placed near where they are used in the program's code, this means that the translator needs access to your code. Most translators do not read programming languages, making it harder for them to recognize what needs to be translated. It also may lead to coding errors if the translators should inadvertently modify your source code.

## Header files

Header files are used to define parts of a program that may be used in multiple places in the code (such as different modules) and may need to be modified often. For example, text strings may be placed in a header file. In this case, the translator is then able to edit the translatable strings in the header file, without having to deal with the core code. To further aid the translator in identifying the translatable text, the header file can be converted into rich text format (RTF) and the translatable text highlighted by changing the font color. The principal drawback in using header files is that the translator may not be able to see the context of the strings they are translating. Without this context information, numerous problems could result for the translator.

## Resource files

Another approach, and one that overcomes the problem specific to header files, is to use resource files (.rc for C++ programming) to isolate your localizable text. Resource files contain the definitions of the dialog boxes, strings, and icons used in your UI. Basically, everything the user sees in your UI can be defined here, making it much easier for translators to understand the context in which the strings being translated are used in the software.

Carrying this process one step further, if you isolate all of your localizable text into resource files that can be compiled into dynamic link libraries (.DLL files), managing multiple language localization is greatly simplified. You have one executable file that pulls localized resources from the localized .DLL files. To change languages you simply change your .DLL files!

## Web UI programming considerations

Web UI programming benefits from the same processes discussed above. As a developer, you have to think about how to isolate text strings that are going to be displayed on the user screen. Unfortunately, the script languages that are used most commonly in Web interface development are not quite as "handy" in this area. Rather than being able to isolate text in special modules like resource files, you may have to embed your text directly in the script. To make the localization process easier, though, you can use comments to format your script files in a way that readily identifies the localized text. Then, your localization vendor can create filters that identify and "mark up" the text for localization.

**In a Bed & Breakfast in France, guests were asked to:** *Please avoid coca watering, cream cleaning, wet towels wrapping, and ironing drying.*

**In a Tokyo hotel:** *Is forbitten to steal hotel toweles please. If you are not person to do such thing is please not to read this notice.*

## Text expansion

Most languages require more characters (and/or words) to represent the same thought being expressed in English, leading to expansion of text strings. The size of text strings is important from two perspectives:

- **Programming language and operating system restrictions**: Now that most development is for 32-bit or higher operating systems, string lengths are no longer restrictive, but keep in mind that string resources are limited to 255 bytes for 16-bit operating systems. If the English string is close to this limit, the translated string is most likely going to be over it! There are ways to create strings longer than 255 characters, but they require re-coding the resources. For example, a string that exceeds 255 bytes can be moved from the resource file to the executable source code and declared as an array, each element in the array having less than 255 characters. The elements of the array are combined to create messages that can exceed 255 characters. For example, the code:

```
char gszFileExtractError [ ] =
"An error occurred while extracting or decrypting
        files from the encrypted container!"
… {a line of text for each element in the array}
"Please contact your distributor or reseller for
        a valid container for reinstall" ;
printf ("ERROR:%d", gszFileExtractError);
```

  defines the array gszFileExtractError that contains a text string in each array element. The printf function then prints all of the characters from the array elements as one message—even if the message itself exceeds 255 characters (as long as the individual elements do not exceed 255 characters).

- **Dialog box control sizes**: Text expansion also affects the design of your program's UI. A button that is sized for the word "Close" might not be big enough to fit the German translation "Schließen." During the localization process (discussed later), buttons and menus can be redesigned to handle the expanded text. This can be avoided, though, by simply planning ahead for text expansion when designing the UI.

## Use comments in your code!

Comments should be used to clarify ambiguous strings by telling a linguist how many characters may be used in a string and how that string is to be used. A programmer neglecting to use comments may write:

```
#define SPS_SPOOLDIR_TITLE "Spool directory"
#define SPS_REMOTESPOOLDIR_TITLE "Remote Spool directory"
#define SPS_SETUP_DEF_FONT
  "F3FF000000000000BC02000000000030201224172696C006300
  63000007000080266F071B04B026B4A7321939070F070020"
```

Without any comments it is impossible to tell how SPS_SETUP_DEF_FONT is to be used. A comment detailing where and how the font definition is used would greatly aid the localization process.

## Special formats

Many European languages use commas instead of decimal points and a period or space instead of a comma to indicate the thousands place. For example, the same number (5134) is represented three different ways in the US, Italy, and Sweden:

| | |
|---|---|
| US | 5,134 |
| Italy | 5.134 |
| Sweden | 5 134 |

Your software must support these variations or you could have a major problem when someone deposits five thousand Deutsche Marks and is credited for five dollars!

In addition to conventions in numbering, nearly every country has a different symbol for their currency and whether this symbol appears before or after the amount also varies. Some examples include:

| | |
|---|---|
| American Dollar | $ or US$ |
| U.K. Pound | £ |
| Japanese Yen | ¥ |
| Deutsche Mark | DM |
| European Euro | € |

***Instructions on a packet of convenience food from Italy:***
*"Besmear a backing pan, previously buttered with a good tomato sauce, and, after, dispose the cannelloni, lightly distanced between them in a only couch."*

## Date and time formats

The date and time formats can vary from country to country. Some countries like the US use the twelve-hour clock while many European countries use a twenty-four hour clock:

| | |
|---|---|
| US | 9:35 PM |
| Germany | 21.35 |
| French Canada | 21 h 35 |

Similarly, the formatting of dates varies by country. The American standard for dates is month, day, year (MM/DD/YY) with various types of separators (/, -). The European standard is day, month, year (DD/MM/YY) with a few exceptions. The Chinese standard is year, month, day. Here are some examples:

| | | | |
|---|---|---|---|
| US | January 14, 1999 | 1/14/99 | 1-14-99 |
| Japanese | 1999 年 1月 14日 | | |
| France | 14 janvier 1999 | | |
| Germany | 14. Januar 1999 | 14.1.99 | |
| Italy | | 14.1.99 | |
| Sweden | 99-14-01 | | |

Even determining which day is the first day of the week can vary! For example, in America the first day of the week is Sunday; however, the French calendar begins each week on Monday.

Abbreviating the days of the week should be avoided since some languages have the same first letters for all the days of the week. Most native operating systems have formatting routines to help with dates and times.

## Units of weight and measure

Most of the world outside of the US uses the metric system; therefore, international software must be able to handle metric measurements. Problems with units of measure are particularly acute in engineering and scientific software where "rounding-off" inaccuracies during the conversion process can have dire consequences. Great care should be taken to ensure correct conversions between English measurements and metric measurements. Remember the Mars Lander debacle that resulted in a failed Mars exploration project? It all came down to bad conversions between English and metric measurements.

# It's all in the details

## Hotkeys

Most programs have hotkeys (keyboard shortcuts) for various tasks. For example, in MS Word, pressing the Control (CTRL) and "F" keys simultaneously opens the "find" dialog box so the user can find a word or expression in the document. The hotkey CTRL+F is "shorthand" for using the mouse to select Edit/Find from the menu in Word.

Quite often, when translated, these hotkeys are no longer appropriate and must be changed to some key from the translated text. For example, when "Close" is translated to "Schließen" the hotkey ALT-C should change to ALT-S. The new hotkeys should be compared in the native operating system environment to make sure that all the hotkeys are unique. Interestingly, for Japanese, Korean, and Chinese, the English hotkeys are retained in parentheses after the translation!

## Composite strings

One of the biggest challenges in software internationalization is coping with composite messages. Composite messages occur where two or more strings are combined to create one message. Composite messages typically have the following format:

```
"The %s has an error: %s"
```

In this composite, the %s would be replaced with text:

```
"The hard drive has an error: out of space"
```

When a translator works with composite strings, there is no way of knowing what the gender of the noun is in the case of %s symbols. The order of each %s cannot change without a programmer altering the code, but the grammatical requirements of some languages might necessitate a change in word order. This complexity could lead to sentences reading like:

```
"The out of space has an error: hard drive."
```

One way of addressing the problem of word order during localization is to use a function to order parameters. This allows the reordering to take place in a header file instead of in the code. If you are using 32-bit Windows, word order can be fixed by using the FormatMessage() function with the %1 and %2 text parameter system, for example:

```
#define STR_ERROR "the $1s has an error $2s"
...

...
sprintf(OutBuf, StrParam(STR_ERROR, device, errormsg))
```

**TIPS**

If you are customizing templates or creating scripts yourself, keep your target languages in mind. Isolate any text requiring localization so that your vendors can easily find it.

## Plural constructions in composite messages

Rules for creating plural constructions differ from language to language. Even in English, the rule for constructing plural nouns is not universal: the plural for "bed" is "beds" but the plural for "leaf" is not "leafs." The following example illustrates the problem with plurals. Take the string:

```
"%d program%s searched"
```

and the string:

```
"%d file%s searched"
```

If %d is greater than one, and the %s is used to insert an "s" to form a plural construction then the message could read either:

```
"1 program searched" and "1 file searched"
```

or

```
"3 programs searched" and "3 files searched."
```

This may work for English but it won't work for the Dutch and for most other European language translations:

| | | |
|---------|---|-------------|
| program | = | programma |
| programs | = | programma's |
| file | = | bestand |
| files | = | bestanden |

In internationalizing your software, it is best to avoid these constructs all together.

## Using the correct character codes

Localized operating systems use different character sets or code pages. Character sets are maps of characters used in the operating system. Some UNIX systems use a 7-bit ASCII character set that only contains 128 characters (including tabs, spaces, punctuation marks, symbols, upper and lowercase alphabetical characters, numbers, and line returns). The 7-bit ASCII character set is too limited for most foreign languages, as it does not contain special characters (such as é, å, or â). A newer standard is 8-bit or "extended" ASCII, allowing 256 characters. Microsoft Windows uses 8-bit ASCII character sets, and for UNIX computers there is an ISO standard (ISO 8859-X). The Microsoft and ISO standards are very similar.

Even with 256 characters the 8-bit ASCII does not have enough space for all the characters used by all languages. To solve this problem there are several different 8-bit ASCII character sets that contain all the characters for a group of similar languages. Japanese, Chinese, and Korean have too many characters in their language to fit in just one extended ASCII character set. For these languages, 16-bit character sets (double-byte, multiple-byte, or variable-byte) are used. In an effort to simplify matters, the character encoding called Unicode was developed. Unicode is a 16-bit code page that contains the characters for almost all languages. Unicode is now being supported on newer operating systems (such as Windows NT 4.0, Windows 2000, and UNIX variants).

## Designing for right-to-left languages

Some languages, like Arabic and Hebrew, read from right-to-left rather than left-to-right. These languages also often contain number strings and/or English text that are written left-to-right. So, there is a combination of left-to-right and right-to-left text on the same page or display. This combination is referred to as "bi-directional" text. The interfaces for these languages put menus and buttons on the opposite side of the screen: menus start on the right, scroll bars are on the left and bottom of the window, and buttons usually appear on the left side of the window. Most of this is handled by rearranging controls in the resource files, but the resources for right-to-left and left-to-right cannot be shared. Any special functions or third-party controls and software should be examined very early in the development process to ensure that they can handle right-to-left languages and bi-directional text.

## Understanding the user's keyboard

In order to input special characters (such as é, á, õ, etc.), each language has a corresponding keyboard. These keyboards make it easier to type most special characters, but some characters that are used often in the US may be more difficult to enter. For example "\" in most Eastern European countries is Right ALT+Q (there is a difference between the right and left Alt keys), and several European languages like German switch the position of the "z" and "y" keys. The Japanese, Chinese, and Korean keyboards require multiple keys to be pressed to create one character. It is important to keep this in mind when choosing hotkeys, or keyboard controls.

**TIPS**

Don't use graphics that have a cultural bias. That cute bunny rabbit might make an American think your product is fast but someone else might think it is dinner!

**Willy van Grunsven**

*"Being Dutch is synonymous with being innovative and adventurous. These qualities have proven to be my lifeline to sanity on one or two occasions in this industry. In all the years that Lingo Systems has been in existence, there have been times that the old story of the little boy holding his finger in the dike to keep the country from flooding has seemed strangely familiar. But more often, Lingo Systems can be more accurately compared to the "Golden Ages" that my country went through in the Middle Ages—a time of richly abundant opportunities and deeply felt, long-lasting relationships. I am very proud of all the wonderful accomplishments of everyone who has worked with us."*

# Text Manipulation
## Hard-coded characters

When writing an application, it is sometimes necessary to search for a specific character. If this character is hard-coded, a change in the code page (to support a particular language) requires a corresponding change to the source code references to the character. For example, the following code makes a direct reference to a hard-coded character:

```
/* search for specific character */
if (current = '¥')
ProcessLine();
```

The "¥" in the original code page is replaced with " Ą " when the code page is changed to the Eastern European (Czech, Hungarian, Polish, etc.) character set. As a result, "¥" cannot be relied upon as a marker to determine when ProcessLine() should be executed. This is not a unique case, as "£" changes to " Ł " in the Eastern European character set, and "Ј" in the Cyrillic character set, making both unreliable markers. Hard—coded characters should be replaced with characters that can be easily redefined if there is a conflict.

## Foreign sort orders

Sorting alphabetically is easy for the US and UK markets, but for other languages how do you alphabetize words with accented characters like é, õ, and à? For most European languages, the accented character is considered the same as the unaccented character and is sorted accordingly (or it follows the unaccented character). Most Scandinavian languages put their accented characters after the z (y, z, æ, å). In Norwegian and Danish, double vowels like "aa" come at the end of the alphabet. In Spanish—speaking Latin American countries "ch" is considered a single character which appears between "c" and "d." Consideration of sort order should be made at the design stage to ensure that your software functions as you intended.

## Uppercase or lowercase?

In your code, determining whether a character is uppercase or lowercase must be treated carefully. There are several tricks you can use to determine if a character is upper or lowercase. The following code is an example of a "quick" way to check if a character is uppercase by determining if it is greater than or equal to "A" and less than or equal to "Z":

```
If ( (Unknown >= 'A') && (Unknown <= 'Z') ) UpperC = TRUE;
```

While this technique works for English, the special characters found in foreign alphabets are beyond the specified range. All special characters would be found to be lowercase because they fall outside the range (even if they are uppercase). Similar problems may be encountered with tests used to determine if a character is alphanumeric or some other symbol.

# Double-byte enabling

It is often necessary for the program to find the length of a string. The most common technique (the function "strlen") is to count the number of bytes in a string. A byte a group of bits (binary 1s or 0s) that are used to create a character. Most languages can be represented with a single byte of information. Japanese, Korean, and Chinese characters, though, are represented by one or two bytes.

These double-byte languages create problems when counting bytes to determine the number of characters in a string. When writing programs for use in these countries, there are different functions that must be used. If you are looking for the length (number of characters) of a string then use the "mbsXXX()" functions. If you are looking for the size (number of bytes) of a string, then use the "strXXX()" functions. Remember, as well, that any strings or arrays must be of sufficient size to handle two bytes per character. For example:

```
#define MAXSTRLEN 10
#ifdef _DBCS
#define MAXCHARSIZE 2    /* two bytes per character */
#else
#define MAXCHARSIZE 1    /* single byte per character */
#endif
int   numofchar;
int   numofbytes;
char  outBuf[MAXSTRLEN * MAXCHARSIZE];
...
...
numofchar = mbslen(outBuf);
numofbytes = strlen(outBuf);
```

All functions used must be examined to see if they can handle double-byte characters.

There are also other issues that should be considered for double-byte languages. Japanese and Chinese (and Thai as well, though it is a single-byte language) do not use spaces between words or characters. This can cause problems with line wrapping.

**TIPS**

When selecting fonts, simpler is better. Ornate or decorative fonts should be avoided, as they impair the legibility of some languages containing special accents and characters.

With the latest Windows operating systems (Windows 95/98, Windows ME, Windows NT, and Windows 2000), multi-language support allows you to view Chinese and Japanese characters on an English system. Third-party software packages allow you to both view and input double-byte text (Richwin, Cstar, Twinbridge, NJWin, etc.). If you are trying to search for specific characters, remember that some single-byte characters like "/", "[", and ">" might be half of a double-byte character. Also, DOS filenames are "8 BYTES dot 3 BYTES," not "8 characters dot 3 characters." For double-byte characters, that leaves you with "4 characters dot one character" for the file name.

**Note**: most double-byte character sets include some single-byte characters and a copy of the English character set.

# Software localization

After successfully completing your software internationalization (planning for issues like text expansion, double-byte enabling, etc.), the software product is ready for localization. The localization process involves several basic steps that are applicable to all types of software projects. The details may vary, of course, depending upon the type of software being localized. Your localization vendor should work closely with you in determining the exact processes that are required for your project.

**The basic steps of a software localization project include**:

- Establishing a configuration management system that keeps track of each of your target language versions of source code,

- Identifying and extracting the text strings in the source language to be localized,

- Translating the extracted strings into the target language(s),

- Reinserting the translated strings into the correct source code version for the target language,

- Testing the translated software, editing the screen display as necessary to accommodate the translated text,

- Performing a linguistic review of the draft version of the localized software to ensure both form and content are correct, and

- Incorporating any final comments and finalizing the product for delivery.

Each subsection below examines the localization process for the three principal software project areas: User Interface (UI), Online Help, and Web sites.

# User interface (UI)

No matter the programming language used for software development, there is typically a way of isolating text strings and dialog boxes that appear on the screen on the UI. Using Microsoft C/C++ as an example, resource files (.rc) are preferably used to isolate these strings (as discussed above under Internationalization). These resource files can be compiled to create dynamic link libraries (.DLL) files for each of the target languages.

The UI localization process requires the resource files (such as the .rc files in Microsoft C/C++) to be treated so that the linguists can easily identify those strings that require translation. There are tools available, both proprietary tools developed by localization firms and third-party tools, that assist in this string extraction process. Depending upon what tool is being used, the resource files are usually handled in one of three different ways:

- Strings are extracted from the resource files completely, being placed in a word processing document with pointers to their original placement in the resource file. Propriety tools often work in this way. Once the localized strings are reinserted into the resource file, the dialog boxes, menus, and graphics are modified to fit the new strings. The main advantage of this process is the automated extraction and reinsertion of the text requiring localization. On the negative side, the linguist, who is working only with the extracted strings, may not see the context in which the strings are being used.

- Resource files are treated so that text strings are highlighted to aid the linguist in identifying them in the resource file. The linguist ignores all of the "code words" in the resource file. Using this process, the linguist can see the entire resource file (though only the text strings are highlighted for editing). As a result, the context of the string can be determined—if the linguist has some experience with reading these files. The localized resource files are then modified by software engineers to edit and resize dialog boxes, menus, and graphics for the translated text. This technique is usually the easiest to implement, as the linguist requires only minimal familiarization with the resource files.

- Some third-party software programs provide a UI that displays the text strings requiring localization. A good example of this type of software is Corel's Catalyst. The linguist works through the software package to access the UI components, translating the text strings into the target language. The software handles the reinsertion into the resource file, DLL, or executable automatically. These tools often provide graphical editors for resizing dialog boxes and buttons as the translation is performed. These systems perhaps offer the most linguist-friendly approach for the localization process, in that the strings and the UI are both displayed for localization and modification.

  Problems may arise, though, as each linguist requires an understanding of the software engineering involved and access to the localization tool. Linguists are paid to translate words, not to do engineering, so they may not be as comfortable with this approach!

**TIPS**

Design your documents with plenty of white space to allow for text expansion during translation. As a side benefit, white space improves legibility and streamlines the formatting/desktop publishing process.

## Donald Arney

*"Raised in the Midwest,
Nebraskan Donald
Arney doesn't speak any
foreign tongues and his
passport is bereft of
exotic border stamps.
After a career of flying
jet planes on missions
of medical mercy, he
took a few years off to
tag endangered sharks.
Now, whenever he isn't
rescuing kittens from
burning barns, he
dabbles in the writing
of fiction."*

# Online documentation

Software packages use various forms of online documentation for user support. At the very least there is normally a "readme" or release notes file. With the advent of multimedia, software manufacturers are increasingly providing other documentation with their software. Some manufacturers have even eliminated printed materials and are relying solely on online documentation.

The two most common examples of online documentation are Help files (typically accessed through the program itself) and online manuals (for user manuals, installation guides, etc.).

## Help Files

Help files are the most common form of online documentation. Microsoft has two standards for Windows Help files: the RTF based WinHelp, and the HTML based HTMLHelp. WinHelp has been used since Windows 3.0, while HTMLHelp was released in August 1997 and is becoming increasingly popular for the Windows 98, Windows 2000, and Windows Me operating systems.

Most WinHelp files are written using tools like RoboHelp (now called eHelp). When translating help files, the localizer needs:

- Source content files (.RTF, .DOC, or .HTML), containing the bulk of the help file text,

- Project files (used to compile the help content),

- Bitmaps or other graphics that are used in the help files (often containing text that requires translation), and

- Other content files (such as the .CNT file used to create the table of contents for the help file).

It is also possible to use macros in help files. These macros should be examined to see if they work in the native operating system. For example, the following macro opens the printer's control panel:

```
ExecProgram("control.exe printers", 0)
```

When used in Windows 9X, nothing needs to be changed to make this work on non-English operating systems. But for Windows 3.1, the "printers" part of the macro needs to match Microsoft's translation of that section of the control panel:

```
French ExecProgram("control.exe Imprimantes", 0)
German ExecProgram("control.exe drucker", 0)
Dutch ExecProgram("control.exe printers", 0)
```

## Adobe Acrobat (PDF) files for online manuals

Another very popular form of online documentation uses Adobe Acrobat to create PDF files. Acrobat is a cross-platform electronic documentation distribution format, providing 100% graphic, font, and page layout fidelity on a variety of operating systems. With Acrobat, documents are viewed as the authors originally intended on virtually any computer platform. Additionally, Acrobat has hypertext links that make document navigation easy and its multimedia capabilities allow authors to include sound and video.

Adobe Acrobat consists of three programs: Reader, Exchange, and Distiller. Reader allows a user to view, search, and print but not to create documents. Exchange offers the user all the features of Reader plus the ability to edit and annotate documents. Distiller allows authors to produce Acrobat documents as PDF files (Portable Document Format). A PDF file is created from PostScript printer files originally generated in some other application (such as Word, PageMaker, Quark, etc.). A PDF file can be generated from any program that can produce a PostScript file.

For a translator to be able to work with online documentation using Acrobat, they need the source files. The source file is translated and then converted into PDF afterwards. The PDF file is then sent to the copy editor and proofreader. Using Acrobat Reader and Exchange, the copy editor and proofreader can edit the translation even if they do not own the source application.

## Single source considerations

Just as single source content management strategies have affected the documentation development world, their impacts are felt in online documentation. Today, it is possible to create content in a desktop publishing software package and then use third-party software to convert this content into Web site files and Windows Help files—all from the same content. The localization of this content becomes a hybrid approach, then, of documentation localization and engineering localization. Typically, the content can be localized directly and then the final file formats (be they PDF, HTML, or Help files) are "engineered" to verify compatibility on native operating systems.

**TIPS**

In designing your software for localization, try to keep all of your User Interface text and dialog boxes isolated in resource files. This way your software can be localized without having to manipulate your functional source code.

**Cory Whitney**

*"OK, so no one ever says, "I want to be a Localization Engineer when I grow up" ...
But, for someone raised by hippies in the back-water woods of New Hampshire, I guess things turned out well enough."*

# Web sites

The use of Web sites continues to grow in leaps and bounds. In business, these sites typically focus on three areas: Marketing, Sales, and Information Management for shared data across corporate Intranets.

Until recently, most Web pages were presented in English. As use of the Internet increases internationally though, more and more companies are considering localization of Web site content.

There are important issues to consider before embarking on a project of Web site localization. Web sites, by their very nature, encourage the site hosts to update and/or modify the information frequently—visitors to the Web site expect to see up-to-date information. It is this expectation that makes localization of Web sites a bit more challenging. A change to one Web page on the site requires changes to the same page in all languages supported. Clearly, Web site maintenance becomes more complicated with each language supported.

Before localizing a company-wide Intranet (with international offices) Web site, you should consider:

- How many foreign staff members use your Intranet?

- Do they require text in their native language?

- Could certain key pages be localized while leaving the bulk of the site in English?

Similarly, the decision to localize your marketing and sales pages, targeted for your specific market, should be carefully evaluated. While localizing the Web site makes your product more visible in a foreign market, you should be sure that your foreign audience is large enough to support the costs for localization and ongoing maintenance of the pages. As with Intranet considerations, it may be possible to localize a subset of your pages to keep costs down while still recognizing your global market.

Cost concerns aside, it is clear that some level of Web site localization is desirable for many businesses. The following subsections address the localization process for Web sites.

## HTML localization process

The complexity of localizing HTML pages for a Web site falls roughly in between that of document and software localization. That is, more engineering support is required than is typically needed in document localization but a bit less than that required for software localization.

Before localization can proceed, the Web site must be evaluated for complexity. Web pages are comprised of content (text), graphic objects, hyperlinks, and advanced engineering features. Each of these components requires consideration in the localization process.

## Web text and graphics

Fortunately, most of the content of a Web page is typically text and graphics. As with the preceding discussion on documentation localization, the same rules apply. It is important to remember that HTML pages have some text that is not immediately apparent, for example:

- Page titles, that appear at the top of the browser interface,

- Graphic titles, the ALT attributes that appear when graphics are loading or when users choose not to downloaded the graphics, and

- Hyperlink titles.

Graphic objects on a Web site that contain text are also normally localized. To avoid having to edit the graphics objects (a more complicated process than text editing), text objects should be separated from the graphic. Text can always be superimposed on a graphic using absolute positioning for graphics and text under DHTML.

**On the menu of a Polish hotel:** *Salad a firm's own make; limpid red beet soup with cheesy dumplings in the form of a finger; roasted duck let loose; beef rashers beaten up in the country people's fashion.*

*The Dairy Association's huge success with the campaign "Got Milk?" prompted them to expand advertising to Mexico. It was soon brought to their attention the Spanish translation read "Are you lactating?"*

## Hyperlinks

Hyperlinks on a Web page have the potential to take users to nonlocalized regions of your Web site or to Web sites of others that are not localized. It may be necessary to modify these hyperlinks so that alternative sites are selected (if available in the appropriate language), or an explanation given in the target language that these sites are in English.

## Advanced Web features

Web sites are increasingly exploiting advanced features to provide more dynamic Web pages. As the pages become more dynamic, the potential for complications in localization increases. CGI script, Java code or script, and ActiveX applets all need to be examined to determine any impacts they may have on the localization process. Ideally, the same standards for software internationalization are applied to any code or scripts that are included on the Web site—simplifying the localization process. As with software projects, any text strings used in the script must be identified for the localization process. Fortunately, the amount of text in these code modules is normally quite small and therefore localization is straightforward. Modules must be tested on native language operating systems, though, to assure they function properly.

The most complex addition to the Web arsenal is the database interface. Here, much of the page content is stored in a database and "called up" onto the Web page as needed. For example, if a user asks to see all of the "large" wool shirts that you sell, your database would serve up a list on the Web page of all of the shirts you have in inventory. If this list is localized, then an added level of complexity is introduced to the Web page: the database not only must serve up the list of shirts, but the right localized list of shirts, and that list must fit correctly onto the page. This is typically accomplished by designing the database to handle this added level of complexity with a "by language" table structure. Similarly, the Web style sheet is modified to handle the "by language" text expansion requirements so that the localized content looks correct on the screen.

## Extended and double-byte characters on the Web

Web pages must be able to display "special" characters on computers all over the world. The accented characters that are found in western European languages (French, Spanish, Italian, German, and Portuguese) are relatively easy to display. Most personal computers support the extended ASCII character set required to represent these letters. For HTML, these "special" characters may be represented either by specific HTML codes or by setting the language encoding for the page. For example, an é is represented in HTML as &eacute (an acute accent over the letter e). These special codes are generated automatically if you use an HTML generator with a WYSIWYG interface.

Localizing Web sites into eastern and central European languages, and into double-byte languages, is slightly more complicated as their character sets are completely different. Fortunately, the browsers from Internet Explorer and Netscape, Version 4 and higher, support language-encoding metatags. As long as the user's PC has the appropriate language support (available as multilanguage support on Windows and Mac platforms), or the native language operating system, the extended character sets appear correctly. Both the Web pages and the browser must be configured to support the desired character set. Fonts must also be installed on the computer to view these double-byte languages.

Using the HTML <META> tag element, the character encoding necessary to view a particular page can be set automatically. For example,

```
<META http-equiv="content-type" content="text/html;
charset=big5">
```

indicates that the page is encoded for Traditional Chinese.

**Sign in a Moscow hotel:** *The passenger must get free the room before two o'clocks of the day they are abandoning in other case, as the passenger fracture the day and must the administration pay for full.*

**Sign in another Moscow hotel:** *Ladies requested not to have children in the bar.*

**From a sign outside of a Roman doctor's office:** *Specialist in women and other diseases.*

## Roger Thompson

*Roger, seemingly only a lead formatter and art director, searches for a way to tap into the hidden strengths that all translations have. An accidental overdose of text files alters his body chemistry. So that now, when Roger grows angry or outraged, a startling metamorphosis occurs. The Creature is driven by rage and pursued by a project manager on a tight deadline.*
*"Mister McGee, don't make me angry.*
*You wouldn't like me when I'm angry."*
*The Creature is wanted for a typo he didn't commit. Roger is believed to be dead, and he must let the world think that he is dead, until he can find a way to control the raging spirit that dwells within him...*

# Software localization quality assurance

## Testing

### Validating the translation

Computers cannot currently fully process the complexities of human languages. To ensure that the software UI appears correctly on the screen and is grammatically accurate, the software text must be reviewed for correctness by a native-quality linguist. Typically the most thorough review is one that is done during or just before regression testing the finished software.

## Testing the localized application

The localization process itself should not lead to the introduction of new defects into the application. However, if the application is not fully internationalized, and code changes are required during the localization process, the potential exists to introduce new functional defects. To be sure that there are no internationalization defects in the application, the localized versions must be tested on a computer configured with the native operating system. A full regression test on newly localized applications should be considered a mandatory step. The localization service most often performs this testing, but the engineering group that constructed the application can also be involved to insure the tests are as complete as possible.

## Functional testing and in-country review

Ideally, to verify that your software has been correctly localized, the final draft of the application should be tested in real-life scenarios on a native operating system. This can be done by your localization vendor or by your in-country representatives. This may involve the use of your international distributors, in-country user community, or native-quality linguists to perform the final review before your product is released to market.

**A construction company brochure from Belgium:**
To enjoy Belgium in the most appropriate way, what could be better than a spacious, modern and cordial full foot or one-storey home. Our country has many construction firms, but some are specialised in the formula "key turn estates". Is.Co.Pan is a dynamic firm who not only take care of finding a suitable parcel of ground, but also take care of the architecture, building licences and loons, and that needs to be done in order to build a home. Therefor they are using a good team of craftmenship and the best material available.

**A sign posted in Germany's Black Forest:**
It is strictly forbidden on our black forest camping site that people of different sex, for instance, men and women, live together in one tent unless they are married with each other for that purpose.

**Maria Falasca**

*"I have a typically
American ethnic
background: Italian,
German, Scots-Irish,
and French Canadian,
which explains my urge
to sing "O sole mio"
while dancing a jig. I
guess it's also the
reason I feel at home in
Lingo's multicultural
environment. I love
languages and get a kick
out of communicating
with our linguists who
are all over the world."*

# What to Look for in a Translator

Does localization mean the same as translation? Can any bilingual person localize materials?

The answers are no and no!

Localization goes beyond translation, to the meaning behind the words that are being used. Different cultures use different grammar and sentence structures, so straight word-for-word translations are never enough to convey understanding. Instead, the form of the source language must be replaced with the form of the target language while maintaining the original meaning and style of the source materials.

The art of localization is complex. An experienced translator can take the essential information from the source material, including register (tone, style, formality, complexity, etc.) and carry it over to the target language translation. Quality of localization is directly linked to the translator's experience with the topic and knowledge of both the source and target languages.

Being bilingual is only the beginning. So just what does it mean to be a translator?

A translator provides native-quality translations. Native quality means that the material, once translated, reads as though it was originally written in the target language. This usually requires the expertise of someone who was raised and educated in the target country. Of course, there are others with exceptional education, training and experience in a specific language who can also provide native-quality work, but it takes true talent.

A translator must have:

- Native fluency in the source language,

- A thorough understanding of the target language,

- Excellent writing skills, including a grammatical mastery of the target language and knowledge of various writing forms and styles,

- Familiarity with current terminology in the desired field. (Experienced translators often find it helpful to maintain extensive reference libraries.),

- A working knowledge of the localization process,

- Access to appropriate tools such as up to date computer models and multiple software applications, and

- An awareness of cultural differences and language subtleties.

Translators must have extensive education. Technical translators require additional experience in order to work in specific fields. Lingo Systems expects the following criteria be met when evaluating translators:

- A Bachelor or Master's degree in an appropriate field,

- A minimum of five years translation experience,

- A minimum of three years translation experience with material similar to the source material,

- Translation certifications such as those provided by the American Translators Association, and

- Demonstrated commitment to the profession through professional affiliations.

**A sign in a Swiss hotel:**
*Because of the impropriety of entertaining guests of the opposite sex in the bedroom, it is suggested that the lobby be used for this purpose.*

**Signs in a Belgrade hotel:**

*Let us know about an uneficiency as well as leaking on the service. Our utmost will improve it.*

*Not to perambulate the corridors in the hours of repose in the boots of ascension.*

# Cristina
# Tacconi Johns

*Cristina could speak a foreign language at a very early age - though it was only after she left her native Italy to discover America that she learned to speak English. She expanded her language prowess on the birth of her son Clarence - soon mastering baby talk (but she is still having difficulties understanding what the heck her cat is trying to say). By day Cristina is the mostly mild mannered Quality Assurance Coordinator and Italian Linguist for Lingo Systems, by night a stand-in for the Dark Angel, righting wrongs and sending the bad guys to bed early with no supper.*

# Quality Assurance and Localization

When it is time to choose a localization company for your product, pay close attention to how often you hear the words Quality and Quality Assurance (QA). You should find a vendor that cares as much as you do about carefully reproducing, in different languages, what took you so much time and effort to create in the first place. That is why inquiring about QA procedures is a useful tool in the decision process regarding the selection of your localization vendor. There are many translators and many translation companies on the market, but only a very few of them can consistently maintain high quality standards for their work. Quality Assurance must be implemented in various forms and at each step throughout the duration of a project in order to deliver the final product exactly as you requested.

## Think quality

Even before the translation process begins, remember to make time to schedule a cultural review of your product. The purpose of the cultural review is to identify any concept, text, or graphics in the source document that can lead to problems in the translation. Your localization vendor should be able to send your product to qualified linguists who can then analyze every aspect of the product to identify possible problem areas.

Make sure, in any case, that your source document undergoes a thorough editing pass. A clear English document, grammatically correct and free from inconsistency in terminology usage, is the prerequisite for a good translated product. Some localization companies offer this service; being proactive can save you a lot of time, problems, and money in the long run. It is less costly to have the source product checked by Quality Assurance professionals prior to localization than to have possible problems replicated in multiple languages.

## Quality assurance steps

### Language

To obtain the highest quality of translation, your localization vendor should have a serious and well-documented procedure of qualification for the linguists and the linguistic agencies it is using. Periodically check the performance and results of its linguistic workforce.

Even before sending the files to the translators, your vendor typically requests the development of a glossary (either done by you or by your vendor upon review of your source material). This ensures that all the linguists working on the same projects are using the same technical terminology. It is incredible how much more efficient the process becomes and how much time can be saved this way!

In order to ensure high quality, the linguistic phase of the project should normally include three steps:

- Translation,

- Copy editing, and

- Proofreading,

The translator is the "lead linguist" on the project and is responsible for converting the source text into the target language. The copy editor then reviews, word for word, the translator's work, verifying the accuracy of the translation. Finally, the proofreader examines the final version for consistency and flow of the language.

Another consideration you may want to discuss with your vendor is performing an in-country review. The in-country reviewer evaluates the specifications of your product against the cultural/linguistic elements of the relevant country. Usually this review is conducted by someone familiar with your products (such as representatives or distributors) in the target country.

**Visual review**

Once the formal translation process has come to an end, the Quality Assurance process continues in different forms, depending on the nature of your project.

If your project includes printed materials, the QA reviewers perform visual validation to ensure that everything in the translated document matches the original English text (source document). The QA reviewer validates items such as:

- Completed translation (all items that should be translated are translated and those that should remain in the source language are not translated),

- Consistent font type, style, and size,

- Correct placement and size of graphics,

- Graphic content (making sure there is no "clipping" of graphic or text elements,

- Pagination flow and page numbering,

- Cross-references between text and the Table of Contents and indices, and

- Text indentation and alignment.

**TIPS**

It is very important that the build environment is clearly specified. Sometimes, localization engineers spend a number of hours figuring this out.

This list can expand considerably and is normally customized for every single project, with input from the client. To help your vendor develop the quality guidelines, it is a good idea to provide them with any information that can aid the translation and QA process early in the Localization process. Some examples of helpful items to provide include:

- Terms and names that are to remain in English,

- A list of part numbers for your products, and

- Measurement units to be used in your document (inches/mm, pounds/grams, Cclsius/Fahrenheit, etc.)

**Functional testing**

Just like your printed documentation, any online documentation generated for your products should be validated in a QA review. The two main online documentation types today, PDF files and HTML files, require functional testing. Your localization vendor should be able to perform functionality testing on your products to assure that they function the way they are intended to on the software platforms consistent with your target markets.

Both PDF files and HTML files need to be tested on computers running native operating systems to ensure that the functionality and character displays are correct. Typically, these files are examined for:

- Compatibility with native operating systems,

- Correct display of fonts and graphics,

- Compatibility with appropriate localized Acrobat Reader versions and HTML browsers,

- Correct function of hyperlinks, and

- Clear printing of pages.

This list may be customized with other items, depending upon any advanced features that may be added to the PDF or HTML files.

### Menu Items

*China - Cold shredded children and sea blubber in spicy sauce*

*Vietnam - Pork with fresh garbage*

*Poland - Roasted duck let loose*

*Cairo - French fried ships*

*France - Sweat from the trolley*

*Nepal - Fried friendship*

*China - Dreaded veal cutlet with potatoes in cream*

*Japan - Strawberry crap*

*Japan - Buttered saucepans and fried hormones*

*Europe - Garlic Coffee*

*Cairo - Muscles Of Marines/Lobster Thermos*

*Europe - Sole Bonne Femme (Fish Landlady style)*

*Bali - Toes with butter and jam*

*Japan - Teppan Yaki - Before Your Cooked Right Eyes*

## Clark Hays

*"As a member of the high-profile Quality Assurance Team, my primry contribution is two catch misteaks, in all there various firms. Consistently finding these often stubborn and well-hidden errors requires dedication, focus, and very muscular eyes. My goal is to eventually move beyond the constraints of current Quality Assurance technologies, developing new techniques to actively seek out and destroy mistakes where they live and breed, in the hearts and minds of authors."*

# Same Language, Different Dialect

Winston Churchill once described the U.S. and the U.K. as two countries separated by a common language. In translation, a similar challenge arises when writing for:

- Spanish readers in Madrid versus Mexico City,
- French readers in Paris versus Montreal,
- Chinese readers in Beijing versus Hong Kong, and
- Portuguese readers in Lisbon versus Rio.

## Spanish

The world of technology is fast-paced. Author Alvin Toffler once said, "What was unknown yesterday is old hat tomorrow." As new technologies are implemented, new vocabulary must be "invented" to name it and to explain it. We have to use nouns, and sometimes verbs, in new contexts.

Throughout the world, there are approximately 300 million people who use Spanish as their native language. This fact poses an interesting challenge to the translation and localization of any material, as the language evolves.

Spanish translators find the problem compounded by the fact that they must write for an audience that is found in regions on two sides of the Atlantic Ocean: Latin America and Spain. Although the differences are minimal, there are linguistic variations and peculiarities that characterize several Spanish-speaking countries, the greatest one being pronunciation.

The "glue" that keeps the Spanish language together as one linguistic unit is the Real Academia de la Lengua Española (Royal Academy of the Spanish Language), which sets the standards of the Spanish language for all the Spanish-speaking countries in the world. Their decisions are meticulously observed by those who teach, write, or are in any way involved with the use and implementation of the Spanish language.

However, because the decisions made by the Royal Academy have such a lasting impact, the Academy is painstakingly slow in reaching those decisions. While the arbiters of new terminology may proceed at a very slow and cautious rate, technology races along. Until the Royal Academy decides each issue, the Spanish translator is forced to make his or her own decisions on terminology. Experienced translators are always careful to use terms that are understood by the greatest number of users, regardless of their place of origin.

If Spanish has a regulating body that decides all matters concerning written Spanish (grammar, syntax, spelling, etc.), why do some people believe that there are different kinds of Spanish? As noted above, the greatest differences exist in the way words are spoken, the way certain letters are pronounced (or maybe not pronounced). Thus, in certain parts of Spain the letter "z" is pronounced as a soft English "th" as in the word thin, whereas, in Latin America the letter "z" is always pronounced as an "s" as in Sam. However, whether in Argentina, Mexico, or Madrid, the word *zapato* (shoe) must always be written with a "z". Local differences can also be found in the use of certain nouns—especially those that designate agricultural products: the English say *potato*, Latin America prefers *papa*, and Spain *patata*.

Geography can also play a role in the determination of terminology. Because of the geographical proximity to the United States, some Latin American countries identify more closely with terms used in the United States and "Spanish-ize" the terms. A good example is the word computer. In most Latin American countries *computer* is rendered as *computadora*. In Spain, because of its proximity to France, computer is rendered as *ordenador*, from the French *ordinateur*. That geographical proximity is not always the determining factor can be seen from another example, the English term "*font*". Latin America prefers *tipo* or *fuente*, while Spain has kept the English word *font*.

While these examples compare Iberian and Latin American Spanish, other linguistic differences occur within Latin America. Chile, Columbia, Argentina, and others may identify more closely with Europe than the United States, yet the rule is not hard and fast. The decimal and thousand separators are good examples. Mexico, Central America, and some South American countries use these separators in the same way as the United States (where one thousand twenty is represented 1,020.00). However, Chile, Columbia, and Argentina prefer the European way of expressing separators (where one thousand twenty is instead represented 1.020,00).

Experienced translators avoid colloquialisms and regionalisms used in specific countries. Instead, they use terms that are understood by the majority of readers.

Octavio Paz, Mexican poet and Nobel Laureate for Literature (1990), said that there is really no Cuban, Mexican, Spanish, or Argentine literature. We can take this one step further and say that there is really no Cuban, Mexican, Spanish, or Argentine Spanish. Difficulties with the language exist only to the degree of formal education and sophistication of the speaker, and, by extension, to the reader's degree of formal education and sophistication.

# Portuguese

Nearly 210 million people speak Portuguese throughout the world today. However, the Portuguese that is spoken is not homogeneous. It differs in grammar, pronunciation, and vocabulary among Portuguese speakers in Portugal and in Brazil.

Brazilian Portuguese was not only influenced by native languages such as Tupinambá, but also by the many languages spoken by African slaves. Although some Brazilian words made their way to Europe, most were only used in Brazil. Southern Brazil absorbed a large influx of immigrants of Italian, German, and Japanese descent. These linguistic groups made several contributions to the language spoken in Brazil. Portuguese in Europe, meanwhile, was influenced by the French spoken during Napoleon's occupation of Portugal.

In the twentieth century, the linguistic split between Portuguese and Brazilian increased as the result of technological innovations that required new vocabulary. Unlike the Royal Academy of the Spanish Language, there is no similar "watch dog" to condone adopting new terminology and grammar in Portuguese.

Internet World Magazine published a list in the Brazilian edition that pointed out some of the differences:

| English | European Portuguese | Brazilian Portuguese |
|---------|--------------------|--------------------|
| to access | aceder | acessar |
| default | predefinido | default |
| mouse | rato | mouse |
| screen | ecrã | tela |

There are also grammatical differences and spelling variations between Portuguese and Brazilian Portuguese.

When localizing into Portuguese, keep these differences in mind. Your localization vendor should distinguish between European and Brazilian Portuguese and should use native—quality speakers of the respective countries to localize your product. Although Portuguese speakers from both sides of the Atlantic are able to understand each other, not localizing properly can lead to confusion among your end-users.

# French

Most natives of France are aware that Canadians speak French with a different accent but are quite surprised to discover variations in the written language. French people are not generally familiar with Quebecois customs or history. When Jacques Cartier explored the bay of Saint Lawrence in 1534, there were no translation dilemmas because the native Iroquois were not willing to speak French!

There are now more than six million French speakers in Canada, most of whom are located in the province of Quebec. In the past four hundred years, the French spoken in this region has evolved dramatically due to geographical proximity with English speakers. It is always difficult to maintain the integrity of a language in a country where nearly everyone is bilingual, and where the information you receive is almost always transmitted in two languages.

It is now common for French-speaking Canadians to use English words in their daily life. For example, "une saucepan" does not mean anything to a native of France but would be easily understood by English speakers. Another example is "un flat" which means "flat tire" in Canada, but not in France. Other examples abound, making it clear that terminology differences do indeed exist and must be accounted for in localization.

Many people in Quebec are fighting to gain their independence from Canada, and for some of them, the decline of the French language is a big issue. Canadian philosopher Jean-Luc Gouin has written that the average college student in Quebec is almost a dunce in his own native language. Most would not go that far but nearly all would admit that the French Canadian language is a language in its own right.

What, then, should you know in deciding whether to translate solely into French or to include French Canadian? French Canadians understand any material translated in French since the written language is so similar. If simple understanding is your goal, the expense of translating specifically for that target audience may not be necessary.

However, if you want French Canadians to feel that your product has been custom-made for them, you should translate it into French Canadian. French translators should have their work copy edited by a Canadian colleague if the translation is intended for Canada to ensure "cultural security." Most of the time, the linguistic changes are minimal, but you can then be confident that your product is indeed targeted for Canada. Localizing products in French Canadian and French should be, of course, done at your discretion. But what is your competitor doing?

## Ting Fan

*"Like many Chinese from Hong Kong, I like to eat. I especially enjoy the variety offered in Portland's dim sum restaurants. Among my favorites are the bean curd rolls known as "Siu Mai," the juicy bite-size pork spareribs, and, of course, the delicate and tasty "chicken feet," Despite the name, it is actually a delicious dish. You should try it. Maybe you'll like it. So, what do you want to eat today? Chicken feet?"*

# Chinese

"Can you speak and write Chinese?" This apparently simple question, can be answered by asking in turn "What does the term 'Chinese' refer to? Do you mean Mandarin, Hakka, Cantonese, Traditional Chinese, Simplified Chinese, or…?" It seems that there is quite a bit of confusion regarding what exactly "Chinese" means in regards to both the spoken language and written language. Let's try to clear up some of this confusion.

Several millennia ago, the origin of the Chinese writing system was pictorial. People drew pictures to express their thoughts; in short, to communicate. As you can imagine, this method of written communication was very cumbersome, and became very difficult when trying to express complex thought. Since then, a number of reforms have been initiated to stylize and simplify the manner of writing Chinese. This, in turn, has resulted in a more uniform writing style. There were language reforms as early as the second century BC (during the Han dynasty). Of all the language reforms that were initiated over the past two millennia, none has had a greater impact than the one carried out by the Mainland China government since the establishment of the Peoples Republic of China (PRC) in 1949.

The mid-20th century language reform simplified the characters used in the Traditional Chinese writing system by reducing the number of strokes needed to write a character. The end result is the Simplified Chinese writing system. The PRC and Singapore currently use the Simplified Chinese writing system. Hong Kong and Taiwan use the Traditional Chinese writing system (though the use of Simplified Chinese may now increase in Hong Kong following their integration into the PRC). It is generally easier for a person who knows Traditional Chinese to understand Simplified Chinese characters than a person who knows Simplified Chinese to understand Traditional Chinese characters.

The continuous efforts at language reform introduced the use of the Roman alphabet to "spell" the pronunciation of Chinese characters. The result is the standard Pin Yin spelling system that is widely used in China, Taiwan, and Singapore.

In order for the Pin Yin spelling system to work, there must be a standard spoken language for the Pin Yin spelling system to be based on. This brings us to one of the most important aspects of the language reform—the standardization of the Chinese spoken language. Pu Tong Hua, referred to as Mandarin in most Western countries, and Cantonese, are two of the several major dialects of Chinese spoken language. Mandarin was chosen as the official Chinese spoken language because it was derived from the Beijing (i.e., Peking) dialect, being taught by scholars and used by the government for nearly 1,000 years. Taiwan and Singapore also use Mandarin as their official language. Cantonese, on the other hand, is a dialect widely spoken in the southern regions of China (the Guangzhou and Hong Kong areas).

Although Mandarin is the official spoken language, it is by no means the only language that is used. For day to day conversation, many people still prefer to speak in the dialect of their respective regions. It is not uncommon to find that two people speaking two different dialects cannot communicate verbally, yet if you ask them to write down what they have said, they can communicate because of the standardized Traditional and Simplified writing systems.

So, to answer that first question of "What is Chinese?" we see that it can be thought of as a "blanket term" for several major dialects and two major writing systems.

| Country | Written Language | Spoken Language |
|---|---|---|
| PRC | Simplified Chinese | Mandarin |
| PRC Guangzhou Province | Simplified Chinese | Cantonese |
| PRC Hong Kong | Traditional Chinese | Cantonese |
| Singapore | Simplified Chinese | Mandarin |
| Taiwan | Traditional Chinese | Mandarin |

The next time you hear the question, "Can you speak and write Chinese?" you should first think about what the term "Chinese" really means!

**In a Budapest zoo:**
*Please do not feed the animals. If you have any suitable food, give it to the guard on duty.*

**In a Tokyo shop:**
*Our nylons cost more than common, but you'll find they are best in the long run.*

## What about Japanese and Korean?

To Americans, Chinese, Japanese and Korean may look somewhat similar when they are written. This is because Koreans and Japanese utilize Chinese characters to a certain extent. Koreans, for example, use some Chinese characters to clarify the meaning of some words in addition to "Han-guel", the Korean alphabet based on phonetic sounds. The Japanese, on the other hand, use three different alphabets:

- Hiragana,

- Katakana, and

- Kanji. (The Japanese term for Chinese characters).

The tricky part is that Koreans and Japanese use Chinese characters, but do not necessarily give them the meaning and sound used by the Chinese. This can lead to some confusion.

Japanese and Koreans have their own unique set(s) of alphabets but utilize some Chinese in a written form when necessary. This is why the three languages may look similar to one another when written. Yet, when spoken, the three ethnic groups are said to have nothing in common when it comes to communication. If you were to put the three different ethnic groups together, no one in the respective groups would understand what the other groups were saying. It would be a mistake to think Koreans could understand what the Japanese were saying and vice versa.

Despite the distinction between these three languages, there are also some similarities. Chinese, Japanese, and Korean are composed of double-byte characters, which require special formatting by the production team. For example, while Euro languages can be delivered to the client with standard text flows, Asian languages may require embedded graphics to represent the text boxes.

Also of note is the fact that the syntax of Japanese and Korean phrases are ordered differently from English. Whereas an English sentence typically begins with the subject followed by a verb and then an object, a Japanese or Korean sentence normally begins with a subject followed by an object and ends with a verb. Another difference between these two Asian languages and English is that a thought may be represented in an Asian language as a phrase or a single "word," where the English phrase is a complete sentence.

|  | Japanese | Korean | Chinese |
|---|---|---|---|
| **Alphabet(s) used** | 1) Hiragana | 1) Hanguel | Chinese characters (used in different styles) |
|  | 2) Katakana | 2) Han-ja (Korean term for Chinese characters) |  |
|  | 3) Kanji (Japanese term for Chinese characters) |  |  |
| **Syntax (sentence structure)** | In reverse order of English; Similar to Korean | In reverse order of English; Similar to Japanese | Similar to English |

**From a letter in response to an inquiry about Chinese lodging:**
"*Dear Madam: I am honorable to accept your impossible request. Unhappy it is, I have not bedroom with bath. A bathroom with bed I have. I can though give you a washing, with pleasure, in a most clean spring with no one to see. I insist that you will like this.*"

# Typing Chinese

Now that you know how to distinguish spoken and written Chinese, you may be wondering how people enter Chinese into a computer. After all, you don't normally see a keyboard with all the Chinese characters as keys. With over 10,000 characters, that would have to be an extremely large keyboard.

In order to enter Chinese into a computer, you need an operating system that supports Chinese input. This could be a native Chinese operating system, or some other operating system with built-in support (or with third-party software installed) for Chinese input. There are three general methods of entering Chinese characters: typing, writing, and speaking.

Inputting Chinese by typing means breaking down each ideogram into a series of alphanumeric characters by using defined rules. These rules allow you to create the characters with a standard keyboard. Numerous input methods have been developed since Chinese computing was introduced. Two of the more popular input methods are Chang Jie and Pin Yin. A person using Chang Jie breaks down a Chinese character into alphanumeric. Developed in Taiwan, Chang Jie is the more popular method associated with Traditional Chinese writing. Pin Yin, developed in the PRC, is closely associated with Simplified Chinese. Pin Yin uses phonetics, breaking down a Chinese character by how it sounds.

Comparing the two methods, to enter the word "Chinese" (中文), with Chang Jie, you type in [L for 中 and YK for 文], and with Pin Yin, you type "zhong1 wen2" (where the number at the end of each "word" indicates the tone of that "word"). Despite the initial learning curve for learning the rules of the input systems, when mastered, typing is the fastest and most effective means of inputting Chinese using today's technologies.

Beyond these two methods that rely upon "typing," improvements in technology have led to new methods that do not require the mastery of the rules for input methods. For example, various companies have developed Chinese writing pads that connect directly to your computer. Users can write directly on the pad, where software then recognizes the writing and displays the appropriate character on the screen.

Another means of inputting Chinese comes from the advances in speech recognition technology. Users can speak directly into a microphone connected to a computer. The software then recognizes the phonetics of each word and displays the appropriate character.

These two relatively new alternative methods for the input of Chinese are not without their own drawbacks. First, the interpretation of written or spoken characters is far from perfect. Also, these methods are still generally slower than the typing methods. However, as technology continues to advance, they may one day overtake the traditional typing method and allow a more convenient way of inputting Chinese into the computer.

**Hong Kong Film subtitles:**

*The bullets inside are very hot. Why do I feel so cold?*

*I got knife scars more than the number of your leg's hair!*

*I am damn unsatisfied to be killed in this way.*

*Fatty, you with your thick face have hurt my instep.*

*I'll fire aimlessly if you don't come out!*

*You always use violence. I should've ordered glutinous rice chicken.*

*Take my advice, or I'll spank you without pants.*

*Beware! Your bones are going to be disconnected.*

*How can you use my intestines as a gift?*

*An American T-shirt maker in Miami printed shirts for the Spanish market which promoted the Pope's visit. Instead of "I saw the Pope" (el Papa), the shirts read "I saw the potato" (la papa).*

# Translation and Localization Glossary

### .BMP (BMP)

A standard bit-mapped graphics format used in Windows. Files end with .BMP extension.

### .GIF (GIF)

Graphics Interchange Format. A bit-mapped graphics file format used by the World Wide Web. It features lossless data compression and is best for computer-generated (i.e., nonphotographic) images. Files end with .GIF extension.
*(See also lossless.)*

### .h files

Header files. These are files used in programming (typically C++) to identify and define common items used throughout the program.

### .JPEG (JPG )

Joint Photographic Experts Group. A lossy compression-type graphics format for color files. Can compress files to 5% of their original size with (some) loss of picture quality. Best for photographic images. Files end with .JPG extension.
*(See also lossy.)*

### .PCX (PCX )

A graphics file format used by PC graphics applications. This widely used file format employs lossless compression. Files end with .PCX extension.

### .PDF (PDF)

Portable Document File. A file format created by Adobe Acrobat, primarily for read-only use with Acrobat Reader. Can be edited with the full version of Acrobat. PDF files capture formatting and layout data from files created with another application, allowing others without that source application to view properly formatted documents via Acrobat Reader on any system supported by Acrobat Reader. Files end with .PDF extension.

### .SHG files

Bitmaps with a hotspot overlay.
*(See also hotspot.)*

## .TIFF (TIF)

Tagged Image File Format. Widely used file format for storing bit-mapped images on both PC and Macintosh platforms. Commonly used for scanned images. Files end with .TIF extension.

## ActiveX

A Microsoft program development technology that allows data to be shared among different applications. Conceptually similar to Java, ActiveX has a significant presence in Web-based applications.

## A-Link

A linking macro provided in WinHelp that allows jumps based on keywords rather than specific context strings. A-links do not have to be localized. A-links are never seen by the user and are used only by the help system.

## BinHex

Binary hexidecimal. A widely-used encoding scheme that converts binary data into ASCII characters. BinHex encoding is especially common on MAC platforms. Files end with .HQX extension.

## Bitmap

A graphic for which the color of each pixel is defined by one or more bits (1 bit for black/white, 4 bits for 16 colors, 8 bits for 256 colors, etc.).

## Callout

A small text box referring to an element or feature in a graphic.

## CAT

Computer Aided Translation is a broad term used to describe an area of computer technology applications that automates and assists with the act of translating text from one language to another. CAT tools are highly effective in improving translation productivity and quality (e.g., Trados Workbench and associated utilities).

## CMYK

Cyan Magenta Yellow Black. A color model in which all colors are described as a mixture of these four process colors. CMYK is the standard color model used in offset printing for full-color documents. Also called four-color printing.

## Compiling

Converting a program written in a high-level programming language from source code into object code. Source code must be compiled before it becomes an executable program.

### Computer code

The computer readable code that makes up a program. Also called object code or machine language.
*(See also executable.)*

### Cropping

Trimming the edges of a graphic to make it fit or to remove unwanted parts.

### DBE

Double-Byte Enabling. Re-engineering an original products source code to support the input, display, and manipulation of double-byte language character sets.

### Decompiling

Opposite of compiling. Changing an application from computer code back into source code. Sometimes referred to as reverse engineering.

### Dialog boxes

The rectangular windows used by a program to display information or request information in a Graphic Users Interface (GUI) (Windows or Mac).

### DLL

Dynamic Link Library. A file that contains executable functions or data for applications. Several DLLs come with Windows and are used by many applications, others are written for specific applications. Files end with .DLL extension.

### Double-byte

A character defined with two bytes (16 bits) instead of one byte (8 bits).

### Double-byte enabled

A program that can handle double-byte languages.

### Double-byte languages

Languages that are coded with twice as much information for each character, such as Chinese, Japanese, and Korean.

### DPI

Dots Per Inch. A common measurement of resolution. Most laser printers can print between 300 and 600 DPI.

## Drivers

Specialized programs that allow communication between peripherals (printers, scanners, video cards, etc.) and the computer.

## Embedded graphics

A graphic is known as an embedded graphic if all the information for it is stored in a document and not in a separate file.
*(See also referenced graphic.)*

## Executable

A program that can be run (executed).

## Functional QA

Testing (assuring the quality of) the functioning of a program's GUI.

## Fuzzy logic

A logic that allows the concept of partial truth-truth values between "completely true" and "completely false." Used to create near matches instead of exact matches during searches, and in artificial intelligence programs.

## Globalization

Designing a product that is culturally neutral and can handle translation into any language without being re-engineered.

## Glossary

A list of terms which includes extensive definitions and grammatical configurations.
*(See also terminology list.)*

## HelpQA

An application written by TextCraft that assists in testing help files.

## Hotspot

The part of a graphic in a hypertext document that, when clicked on, jumps to another location. Similar to a hypertext link.

## HTML

Hyper Text Markup Language. A coding system used on the World Wide Web to format text and set up hyperlinks between documents. Similar to SGML.

## HTMLHelp

A new Microsoft standard to replace WinHelp. WinHelp is RTF based, HTMLHelp is HTML based.

### Internationalization

The process of reengineering a product so it can be localized for export to any country.

### ISO

International organization for standardization. A world wide federation of national standards bodies from approximately 130 countries.

### Java

A platform-independent, object oriented programming language. Java can add animation, spreadsheets, and information processing features HTML cannot provide.

### Kerning

Adjusting the space between two text characters. *(See also tracking.)*

### K-link

A linking macro provided in WinHelp that allows jumps based on keywords rather than specific context strings. K-links require translation.

### Leading

Adjusting the space between two or more lines of text. Also called line spacing.

### Leverage

Building current translation projects on those previously completed. Reduces the need to retranslate words and phrases previously translated. The process of using one translation for repeated sections of text.

### Localization

Adapting a software, document, or Web site product to various markets or localities. This may require a variety of steps including translating user interface text, modifying formats for numbers and dates, and replacing culturally inappropriate graphics or system design.

### Lossless

A term used to describe compression techniques that don't lose any data. Lossless compression techniques usually reduce the size of the compressed file up to 50% of the original file.

### Lossy

A term used to describe compression techniques that lose some data or details. Commonly used with graphics and video. Lossy compression techniques can compress files to around 5% of their original size with some loss of data.

## Multiterm

An application made by TRADOS to point out already translated terminology to translators.

## Pixel

Picture Element. One dot on a computer screen. The smallest image-forming unit on a display screen.

## Quality assurance

The process of assuring that the target document resembles the source document as closely as possible. The process can include, for example, verification of layout and graphics to confirm the document is complete.

## Referenced graphic

A graphic that has been placed in a document, in which the information for the graphic is stored in a separate file, and minimal information about the graphic is stored in the document.
*(See also embedded graphics.)*

## Resource files

Source files that contain information to be compiled into the program. They contain the parts of the application that is seen by the user. Typical file types include: .rc, .res, .bmp, .ico, .cur.

## RGB

Red Green Blue. Blending these three colors allows computer monitors to display color images.
*(See also CMYK.)*

## RoboHelp

An application made by BlueSky software. RoboHelp assists in writing help files using Microsoft Word.

## RTF

Rich Text Format. A type of document that encodes formatting as text based tags. Can be opened as text to view the tags or converted to look like a Word document (without the tags visible). Used as a source file for WinHelp.

## Scaling

Changing the size of a graphic so that no distortion occurs.

## Screen shots

A graphic image of what is seen on the computer screen. Often used in user's manuals to show how an application looks on the screen. Also called "screencaps" or "screen captures."

## SEA

Self Extracting Archive. A file that decompresses itself. Used on a Mac OS.

## SGML

Standard Generalized Markup Language. SGML is an ISO (Mac OS) standard for marking text files to show how they should be formatted. HTML is a specialized application of SGML rules.

## Sizing

Changing the size of a graphic. Sizing can cause distortion.
*(See also scaling.)*

## Source code

The human readable code that is compiled to make a program. Some types of source code are C++, Java, HTML (for HTMLHelp), RTF (for WinHelp).

## Source file

A file containing source code that is used to compile.
*(See also source code.)*

## String tags

Tags used in strings to mark where something will be added. For Example: "%s" = another string, "/n" = a return character, and "/t" = a tab, etc.

## Strings

Groupings of characters (letters, numbers, and/or punctuation marks) that are used in programs such as error messages, button labels, etc. Often strings are enclosed in single or double quotes. Strings need to be translated if they contain text that will be seen by the user.

## Terminology list

The terminology list is created as a reference for linguists (translators), and is usually specific to a project. It provides the linguists with the English source word and the target language equivalent. Terminology lists are created by the linguists and approved by the client prior to translation. A list of terms and descriptions are recommended for each specific case.
*(See also glossary.)*

## Text expansion

The increase in the total number of characters that often occurs during translation.

## TRADOS

A German company that creates translation tools. Makers of Multiterm and TRADOS Translator's Workbench.

## TRADOS Translator's Workbench

An application to assist a translator by showing how similarly translated sentences were translated. This software program is used to store linguist-translated text and display it when previously translated phrases appear in a word file. Helps to assure consistency and reduce redundant work.

## Translation

Translation is the process of converting text into another language. Culturally accurate translations convey the total meaning of the source material into the target language, with special attention paid to cultural nuance and style.

## Unicode

A platform independent character set that attempts to unify all character sets into one 16 bit character set. Unicode is a two-byte encoding that allows for 65,536 (256 times 256) code points and includes all major alphabetic languages plus a unified Chinese, Japanese, and Korean character set.

## WinHelp

Short for Windows help file. WinHelp is also the name of the application that runs Windows help files (.hlp).

## Zip file

A compressed file created by the utility application PKzip or WinZip on a PC.

## Zip drive

A 100MB removable media drive made by Iomega.

# Resources

*International Trade Administration,*
*Department of Commerce* . . . . . . . . . . . . . . . . . . . . . . . . . . . . . . . . . . . . . . . . . 202-482-2867

*U.S. Bureau of the Census, Center for International Business Research* . . . . . . . . . . 301-457-1722

*U.S. Department of Commerce (www.stat-usa@doc.gov)* . . . . . . . . . . . . . . . . . . . . . 800-782-8872
      • "A Basic Guide to Exporting"
      • "National Trade Databank" (CD-ROM)

*Trade Information Center, International Trade Administration* . . . . . . . . . . . . . . . . . . 800-872-8723
      • Free telephone consulting with
        international trade counselors. . . . . . . . . . . . . . . . . . . . . . . ***www.ita.doc.gov/tic***

*U.S. Chamber of Commerce International* . . . . . . . . . . . . . . . . . . . . . . . . . . . . . . . . 202-463-5460
      • "Setting up an Office in Japan"

*State of Oregon European Trade Development* . . . . . . . . . . . . . . . . . . . . . . . . . . . . . 503-229-5625
      • Information on localization, licensing, selecting the right
        distributors, and market research. . . . . . . . . . . . . . ***www.craig.burk@state.or.us.***

*Office of European Union and Regional Affairs* . . . . . . . . . . . . . . . . . . . . . . . . . . . . 202-482-5276

*Directory of European Business* . . . . . . . . . . . . . . . . . . . . . . . . . . . . . . . . . . . . 81-466-6152 (UK)
      • The directory is broken down into 33 countries, covering
        both Eastern and Western Europe and the former Soviet Union.

*EU Hotline* . . . . . . . . . . . . . . . . . . . . . . . . . . . . . . . . . . . . . . . . . . . . . . . . . . . 301-921-921-4164

*EU Office - Belgium* . . . . . . . . . . . . . . . . . . . . . . . . . . . . . . . . . . . . . . . . . . . . . . . 32-2295-5724

*British Chamber of Commerce* . . . . . . . . . . . . . . . . . . . . . . . . . . . . . . . . . . . . . . . 415-296-8645
*41 Sutter Street, 303 San Francisco, CA 94104*
      • They have copies of the EU Standards. . . . . . . . . . . . . . . . . www.baccsf.org

*International Business Standards* . . . . . . . . . . . . . . . . . . . . . . . . . . . . . . . . . . . . . . 301-975-2000

# Associations

*American Electronics Association* . . . . . . . . . . . . . . . . . . . . . . . . . . . . . . . . . . . . 800-284-4232

• Software Partners: The Directory of Japanese Software      www.aeanet.org

• Directory of Japanese Software Distributors

• Working with Japan/Working with China (videos)

• The Export Sales and Marketing Manual

• Managing Globally: A complete guide to competing worldwide

• Profiting from Trade Liberalization: AEA Guide to the Uruguay Round

• NAFTA: An Operations Road Map for American Industry

• Standards Making in Europe

*American National Standards Institute (ANSI)* . . . . . . . . . . . . . . . . . . . . . . . . . . . 212-642-4900
11 West 42nd Street New York, NY 10036 . . . . . . . . . . . . . . . . . . . . . . . . . . www.ansi.org

*American Society for Testing and Materials (ASTM)* . . . . . . . . . . . . . . . . . . . . . . . 610-832-9585
100 Barr Harbor Drive West Conshohocken, PA 19428-2959. . . . . . . . . . . . www.astm.org

*LISA* . . . . . . . . . . . . . . . . . . . . . . . . . . . . . . . . . . . . . . . . . . . . . 41-21-821-3210 (CH)
Localisation Industry Standards Association. . . . . . . . . . . . . . . . . . . . . . . . . . . www.lisa.org
7, route de Monastère CH-1173
Féchy, Switzerland

*Society for Technical Communication (STC)* . . . . . . . . . . . . . . . . . . . . . . . . . . . . . 703-522-4114
901 North Stuart St., #904
Arlington, VA 22203-1854 . . . . . . . . . . . . . . . . . . . . . . . . . . . . . . . . . . . www.stc-va.org

*Software Information and Industry Association* . . . . . . . . . . . . . . . . . . . . . . . . . . . 202-452-1600
1730 M Street NW, Suite 700
Washington, DC 20036-4510 . . . . . . . . . . . . . . . . . . . . . . . . . . . . . . . . . . . www.siia.org

*Video Electronics Standard Association*. . . . . . . . . . . . . . . . . . . . . . . . . . . . . . . . 408-957-9270
920 Hillview Court, Suite 140
Milpitas, CA 95035 . . . . . . . . . . . . . . . . . . . . . . . . . . . . . . . . . . . . . . . . . www.vesa.org

# International Computer Societies

| | |
|---|---|
| *Austria* | www.ocg.or.at |
| *Australia* | www.acs.org.au |
| *Belgium* | www.bfia.be |
| *Brazil* | www.sbc.org.br |
| *Canada* | www.cips.org |
| *China* | www.cie-china.org |
| *Czech Republic* | www.cs.cas.cz |
| *France* | www.asti.asso.fr/ |
| *Germany* | www.gi-ev.de |
| *Hungary* | www.njszt.iif.hu |
| *Hong Kong* | www.hkcs.brg.hk |
| *India* | www.csi-india.org |
| *Ireland* | www.ics.ie |
| *Israel* | www.iash.org.il/ |
| *Italy* | www.aica.iol.lt |
| *Japan* | www.ipsj.or.jp |
| *Korea* | www.kiss.or.kr/0menu4_e.html |
| *Malaysia* | www.mdc.com/my |
| *Netherlands* | www.ngi.nl |
| *New Zealand* | www.nzcs.org.nz |
| *Norway* | www.dnd.no |
| *Philippines* | www.pcs-it.org.ph/ |
| *Russia* | www.ras.ru |
| *Singapore* | www.scs.org.sg |
| *Spain* | www.dit.upm.es |
| *Switzerland* | www.s-i.ch/ |
| *Taiwan* | www.mgt.ncu.edu.tw/csim |
| *Thailand* | www.inet.co/th/itweek/tfit.htm |
| *United Kingdom* | www.bcs.org.uk |

# Publications

*ATA Chronicle.* . . . . . . . . . . . . . . . . . . . . . . . . . . . . . . . . . . . . . . . . . . 703-683-6100
Publication of the American Translators Association . . . . . . . . . . . . . . . . . . . www.atanet.org

*Intercom* . . . . . . . . . . . . . . . . . . . . . . . . . . . . . . . . . . . . . . . . . . . . . . . . 703-522-4114
Publication of the Society for Technical Communication. . . . . . . . . . . . . . . www.stc-va.org

*Technical Communication Online* . . . . . . . . . . . . . . . . . . . . . . . . . . . . . . . . . 703-522-4114
Journal of the Society for Technical Communication. . . . . . . . . www.techcomm-online.org

*Language International* . . . . . . . . . . . . . . . . . . . . . . . . . . . . . www.language-international.com

*Latecomer's Guide to the New Europe* . . . . . . . . . . . . . . . . . . . . . . . . . . . . . . 208-263-8178
A handy and concise pamphlet geared to firms
interested in expanding their market into Europe. . . . . . . . . . www.info@multilingual.com

*MultiLingual* . . . . . . . . . . . . . . . . . . . . . . . . . . . . . . . . . . . . . . . . . . . . . . 208-263-8178
319 North First Street
Sandpoint ID 83864 . . . . . . . . . . . . . . . . . . . . . . . . . . . . . . . . . . www.multilingual.com

*Software Business.* . . . . . . . . . . . . . . . . . . . . . . . . . . . . . . . . . . . . . . . . . 720-528-3770
7355 E. Orchard #100
Englewood, CO 80111 . . . . . . . . . . . . . . . . . . . . . . . . . . . . www.infowebcom.com/software

*J@pan Inc.* . . . . . . . . . . . . . . . . . . . . . . . . . . . . . . . . . . . . . . . . . www.japaninc.net
Web site with useful information about doing business in Japan.

## Notes

## Notes

# Notes